Healing ꞁ ꞁ🙰ꞁ🙰🙰🙰

By Jennifer Dent

Healing Homes

©1995 Jennifer Dent

ISBN 1 898307 46 6

ALL RIGHTS RESERVED

No part of this publication may be reproduced, stored in a retrieval system or transmitted in any form or by any means, electronic, mechanical, photocopying, scanning, recording or otherwise without the prior written permission of the author and the publisher.

Cover design by Daryth Bastin
Cover and internal illustrations by Priscilla Clare King

Published by:

Capall Bann Publishing
Freshfields
Chieveley
Berks
RG20 8TF

Tel/Fax 01635 248711

Acknowledgements

For all their help and support I would like to thank Paul and Cilla King, Cilla in particular for the beautiful illustrations, Paul and Barbara Venn-Lever, Christina Shirley, Brian Sumner and my husband, Rik, for his support and encouragement and for his help in editing the book.

Thanks to Dorothy and Howard Sun of Living Colour for their informative and enjoyable courses.

Many thanks to my mother, Joan Griffin, for making my childhood homes so happy, and to Jack Dent for all his help over the past few years.

Finally thanks to Jon and Julia Day of Capall Bann Publishing for all their help and support.

Disclaimer

This book is not intended in any way to be interpreted as prescribing for any illness or other physical or mental conditions.

This book is dedicated
to Gaia -
long may our
home sustain us

CONTENTS

INTRODUCTION

My family moved several times when I was growing up and I lived in a variety of homes. From a caravan to council house, to a charming old white-washed cottage with a huge rambling garden. Unfortunately, when my father bought a business in another town we had to move again and sell the cottage (this was 1961 and the cottage was sold for £100 and demolished to make way for a potato field!). The next house was a brand new semi-detached property, totally devoid of character and a total contrast to the cottage, and finally, to a very substantially built railway gatehouse. This was much more interesting, if somewhat noisier!

All my homes were comfortable, if not luxurious, and more importantly, happy places to live, filled with a lot of laughter and the delightful smells of home baking and flowers from the garden.

When I left home to join the Women's Royal Air Force I lived in a succession of barrack rooms and tiny one person rooms until I married and moved into the comparative luxury of a fully furnished married quarter.

The married quarter, furnished with MOD style furnishings and colours, made me take stock. What on earth was I going to do with it to make it more personal and inspiring?

With time to spare after resigning from the WRAF, this challenge spurred me on to delve into the mysteries of colour, particularly from a psychological point of view, and for good measure I took a correspondence course on interior design. The rest, as they say, is history.

With little money, but a lot of creativity, I made the married quarter into more of a home - a home that fed an inner need I had not previously been aware of.

I realised that whilst we have the need to put our own personal stamp on our surroundings we often lacked the self-confidence to express ourselves fully. However, I always felt that there was more to it than that. A home should not just look good, it should nurture our inner needs as well as the more mundane outer ones, so eventually I studied various aspects of healing; became interested in plants, flowers, herbs and crystals; fascinated by patterns, shape and form, and was intrigued by the effects of light, colour, sound, music and the cycles of nature. This book then is the accumulation of years of interest in all the many aspects that go into the creation of a truly healing home.

I was delighted then, when a few years ago a book was published which brought together many of these aspects. The book was called *The Natural House Book* by David Pearson. A while later I found a book by Carol Venolia, an American Architect, called *Healing Environments* which was an inspiration to me, and it is Carol Venolia I must thank for inspiring the title of my book. As with *Healing Environments*, *Healing Homes* has a double meaning. Not only do we receive healing from such a home, but by treating our homes in this way we also heal our homes.

Home is an abstract concept, it is not merely defined by the building we live in. In one sense our homes help define who we are, and give us stability and identity in a changing world. This is partly why it is so devastating to be made homeless. When we have no home, we appear to become a nobody, to almost cease to exist, and we easily get caught in a downward spiral of despair, apathy and hopelessness.

I have never been homeless, although my husband and I once spent six months, during a winter, living in a 12 foot long caravan on a farm. This had its difficulties, yet I do remember being very grateful every night to have a roof over my head and a reasonably warm bed to climb into, indeed I was more grateful in those humble surroundings than I have ever been before or since. Even basic facilities give you hope and more self respect.

Today the problem of homelessness is a challenge we need to address, and we should be prepared to look at innovative, even unusual and offbeat, solutions, for there must be an answer to this increasingly common problem.

I have written this book for those of us who already live in a home and have to make do with what we have. Whilst I think that the majority of housing in Britain is badly designed, both for the climate and the soul, and is often inappropriate for our needs, this is what we have to work with.

For those of you who have the opportunity to start afresh and build from scratch, I highly recommend that you read *The Natural House Book* by David Pearson, and become familiar with the ecological problems we face today. Not only could you create a building that is ecologically sound and well insulated, but you have the opportunity to use non-harmful, healthier products in your environment. Thus you will have an ideal base to create a superbly healing home. The rest of us will have to work around what we already have, but even so, there is great scope for creating a more healing atmosphere in any home.

There is one thing, however, that is more important than any other factor mentioned in this book, something that nurtures us, heals us and makes our homes truly blessed, and that is love. If the shape of the house is wrong, or the colours around you not quite right, it does not matter if the home you live in is filled with love. But a home filled with love, beauty and a healing ambience, sets the scene for you to lead a happy, healthy and fulfilling life.

Jennifer Dent - April 1995

CHAPTER 1

WHAT IS HOME?   WHAT IS HEALING?

Home is the place where we define our boundaries and express our inner selves. A place to which we belong. A place to be uniquely ourselves, a place of security, of connection, of renewal, of healing, a place to dream. Home, they say, is where the heart is.

A home should by definition connect us with the earth and nature and with the sense of something beyond ourselves. A home is where we exist between birth and death, the final home-coming.

Be it forest, desert, snow, tundra, seashore, river, on the road, in the country, in the town or city, home is the place where we feel comfortable with ourselves. It is our refuge, our sanctuary, a retreat from the world out there. It can be the innermost place of quiet within the mind and soul. Our homes are a reflection of where we know we belong, an artificial construct that fulfils a need either at a most basic level or at a supreme level of nourishment and healing.

It is our sacred space, or temple. The word temple having the same root as temenos, meaning sacred enclosure.

Ultimately that sense of home should be within us, regardless of where we are at any time, but, meanwhile, we can utilise the home environment to provide a structure symbolic of our connections to the outer and inner worlds.

Our homes are multi-layered, with our personal bodies being the most intimate of our environments. Next comes our dwelling place, our house, tent, hut, boat - whatever we utilise for our shelter and protection. Then our community, be it village, town or city, county, country or nation, continent, planet, solar system, galaxy and universe. We inhabit most of these levels at any one time, we may move about from place to place, from country to country, even from continent to continent, but rarely from planet to planet or galaxy to galaxy. So we define our boundaries by knowing where we come from, where we live at the moment, and by our expectation of where we might live in the future.

The purpose of home is not just to keep us warm and safe, but also to protect our beliefs, our values and our personalities. Home gives us a sense of control and order, familiar routines, comfort and relaxation. It forms the setting where our relationships and interaction with friends takes place. We also need a balance between openness and privacy in our homes, particularly at times from other members of the family.

We tend to be creatures of habit, disliking change and being comfortable with the familiar. We continue to surround ourselves with what makes us feel comfortable, sometimes regardless of the fact that the very comfort lies in what our parents found comfortable and reassuring. When we become adults we must awaken to the fact that we have a need to reassess our surroundings as they reflect ourselves and our personality. Do we have the maturity to choose our own colours, our own style, our own sense of self? By so doing we strengthen our ability to choose in all areas of our life and to take back our own personal power, the power to be who we really are.

The structures we have used as homes have been many and various, depending upon our way of life, the climate, landscape and availability of materials to build with. Early humanity, they say, lived in caves, naturally formed in the living rock, or in forests, utilising wood and plants for shelter. Many early peoples were nomadic hunter gatherers and had need for homes that could be dismantled and carried, utilising hides and fibre for tents. It was agriculture that brought about the need for a more permanent type of dwelling and the people mostly adapted a whole range of local materials that usually blended with their environment and responded to their climate. Homes were generally individually craft-built and were appropriate to the people and the land.

The Industrial Revolution finally ended these traditions as the requirement changed to close-packed, urban and anonymous terraces, built as close to the factory, mill or mine as possible. This style of building bought its own problems - overcrowding, disease, lack of sanitation and dark and airless conditions.

Conditions have certainly improved since then, but we never broke away from the mechanised aspect of designing and building homes. In Britain we appeared to lose our vision where housing was concerned and we have inherited a legacy of box type housing. Often draughty, with little insulation, and even less style, we never seemed to allow for the fact that several months of the year are usually cold, wet and windy. At least nearly all houses now have bathrooms and meet certain standards as regards space and safety, but we do not appear to be able to design houses that cater for the soul or spirit.

There are some interesting and well-designed houses about although the general feeling is that they tend to be unaffordable. You could, of course, take the bold step of having a house designed specifically to your requirements. This need not cost as much as you might expect, particularly with the advent of self-build homes such as the those built by the Walter Segal method. These houses do not require conventional foundations and footings to be dug out, nor do they require a level site. They also incorporate a high level of insulation and have a timber frame construction which can easily be built by laymen.

One of the main problems facing the self-builder is finding land to build upon and this may take effort, time and patience to locate.

If you wish to have a house designed for you then you require the services of an architect, ideally one with the vision to create an inspired design and the knowledge and awareness to create an ecologically sound house. In Britain, we now have the Ecological Design Association, an organisation which brings together architects, designers and ecologists.

The ultimate healing home would be designed and built, with the help of the owners, with the awareness of healing principles and much love.

The majority of us, however, have to take what we can find, either buying or renting, and what we usually end up with is a box-like structure within which we have to create our homes. For many people this is a challenge that they meet very well, being fired with enthusiasm to create a home that fulfils their need for self-expression and creativity. We can always improve upon what we have, and most of us do.

We should rejoice in our uniqueness and give full range to our self-expression. We do not have to slavishly adhere to fashion, or to pre-set rules when we choose our fabrics, furnishings and trimmings. Now, as never before, we have an amazing variety of colour and materials to work with, and if we cannot afford to buy new, there are many sources of used furnishings available to us.

Whether we live in a mansion or a one room bedsit, there is always something we can do to personalise our space, to create for ourselves a home, and it is only one step more to make that space, our home, a healing home.

Now we have looked at the concepts of home we can turn to the subject of healing, however, before we look at healing we need to consider what we really mean by good health. For many people good health represents being free from pain, illness and disease and when illness strikes the only thing to consider is to get rid of the problem as quickly as possible, so they can get on with their lives free from the restrictions of ill health.

What is illness? At a basic level it is disorientation and disorder, a disruption of normally harmonious patterns, but why? Modern medicine, since the days of Pasteur, has believed that many diseases are caused by the bacteria and germs in our environment. But why then, do many people stay immune from this assault of bacteria. There are bacteria everywhere, in and on our bodies, in our environment - everything teems with bacteria, so what mechanism allows certain bacteria to suddenly become so harmful to us?

What is happening when we fall ill? Are we perhaps trying to tell ourselves something that we would not let ourselves hear in the course of everyday life. We are beginning to understand the connections between the mind, emotions and the physical body. Negative emotion as well as positive emotion has a definite physical effect. Years ago I remember reading about some tests carried out on people's saliva whilst they were experiencing a particular negative emotion. One stands out in my mind - someone experiencing malicious anger was found to have saliva which contained minute traces of toxins similar to the venom of a poisonous snake. It would appear that our emotions effect us chemically, and eventually those chemicals, and their reactions, have a physical effect.

If negative emotions are potentially so harmful, could we stop being ill if we stopped experiencing negative emotions? Well possibly, but who among us is going to be able to stop experiencing such emotions. If we attempt to do this by suppressing such emotions we would be in even more trouble. It is possible that the way to deal with negative emotions is to let them out when they first spontaneously arise, in an appropriate manner, thus defusing the effect they have when we stuff them into our bodies. A lot of our present day negative emotions are emotions that erupt after a period of suppression, making them even more volatile than they need have been.

We also know that at some stage each and every one of us has used ill health, even unconsciously allowing it to develop, to avoid an issue we do not want to deal with. Or we simply resort to having a cold, for example, because we really do need to rest and distance ourselves from our everyday occupation. It is a real cold, but at some level we know a cold will be accepted as a valid excuse, whereas saying we are going to take three or four days off for a rest would not go down too well.

So there may be many motivations behind certain illnesses and conditions although frequently we are not consciously aware of what is going on or we are unwilling to take responsibility for these motivations.

In fact, we are generally encouraged not to take responsibility for our illnesses. The current paradigm suggests that at the first sign of a disorder we seek outside professional help and relinquish our say in the matter. Now I am not suggesting that we do not go to the doctor - whilst we are living within the paradigm it is important that we do always get things checked out, but we can still accept a measure of responsibility in the process.

So let us look again at good health. Perhaps we need to extend our definitions of good health, not just to include the concept of wellness, but also to include a sense of knowing who, or what, we are, and a true sense of our own self-worth. Knowing who, or what, we are, suggests that we need to at least consider an underlying spiritual dimension to our lives, and a sense of our own true worth would immediately change our lives for the better. So many of us feel under-valued or have a lack of self-esteem which may be as bad for us as being undernourished. Our modern society seems to unknowingly breed lack of self-esteem and we can spend a lifetime trying to compensate for this lack in our lives.

We have also lost an awareness of a sense of connection to something greater than ourselves. This is the spiritual dimension that is so important to us, not necessarily in a religious context, although many people seem to think that religion is the only road to spiritual enlightenment.

We have a reasonably good understanding of the physical, mental, psychological and emotional dimensions but have an inner awareness of something missing. It is as if nothing will ever make sense unless we have a further piece of information. Where do we come from? Where do we go? What is the purpose of life? Why are we here? All questions that trigger a search, or quest if you like, that will reveal the missing something. I cannot give you the answers as we all need to search for our own truth but what I can do is introduce you to some of the mysteries of the subtle aspects of life and reality. Healing, in its widest sense, deals with many of the subtle aspects of life.

So what is the function and purpose of healing? At the most basic level it is to bring back into balance that which has become unbalanced. The act of healing aspires to suspend the disorder long enough to allow the resonance of health to be re-established, whilst attempting to understand the purpose or meaning behind the disorder.

To enable us to bring back balance at this basic level we first have to establish what this level is. It would appear that this most basic level is the level of energy, vibration and frequency.

We have spent the last few hundred years studying the human body, and more recently, the human mind, but now it is time to discover the secrets of the energy body. Secrets that have been known to different cultures throughout history, particularly by the Indian and Chinese cultures which are both very ancient. Mystics have indicated that all that exists is energy and that matter is an illusion. Modern quantum physics is also beginning to reach a similar conclusion - all that exists is vibrational energy, or oscillating wave-forms that form a web of interconnecting patterns and relationships based on resonance.

When these vibrational frequencies reach a certain level they appear to us to become something else, ie colour becomes sound, sound becomes manifested form, and at some point on that journey these frequencies are able to be 'moulded' by the energy of thought.

Clairvoyants have said for a long time that every living thing is surrounded by an aura of energy. It was thought that every human emanated an energy field, not just of heat, but of a whole range of subtle energies, possibly electo-magnetic in nature, that is visible to clairvoyant sight.

It is now suggested that the subtle energies themselves are, in fact, the blueprint of the physical body. The aura generates the physical body rather than the physical body generating the aura. This leads us to consider that the whole of physical reality is generated by a pattern or blueprint of energy. All is vibration

- the only difference between 'things' is the rate or frequency of their vibration.

We could say then that the human energy system is a field of energy placed in space and time, focused in physical reality. We consist of a whole range of vibrational frequencies, pulsating in beautiful patterns and relationships, full of light and colour.

This energy body appears to interpenetrate the physical and when this energy field, which contains our consciousness, departs from physical reality then our physical 'husks' lose coherence and disintegrate, in other words, our bodies die. Our consciousness, immersed in a sea of vibrational frequencies simply focuses on a different wavelength.

It has been proposed that illness and disease first shows itself, or is caused by an imbalance of some kind, in this subtle energy field. If the problem is not addressed at this level, it eventually manifests in the physical body as an emotional, mental or physical disturbance and may be harder to deal with.

Many forms of healing attempt to work directly on this subtle energy field and this type of healing is often referred to as vibrational healing. Spiritual or psychic healing attempts to work on a vibrational level directly, without the use of tools. Other forms of vibrational healing or therapy use such 'tools' as light, colour, sound, crystals, fragrance, homeopathic substances, flower remedies and essences, to help balance the subtle energies. Whilst doing this many healers and therapists will also endeavour to discover in a caring way, the possible reason behind the imbalance in the subtle energy field, thereby addressing the causes at a fundamental level.

Because we live within a sea of electrical, electro-magnetic energies we obviously have subtle connections with the energies in our surroundings and any place we spend a great deal of time in has a large impact, in more ways than one, on our lives. Our home is one of those places. It is our personalised sea of subtle energy connections, where we have the most say in what we choose to surround ourselves with.

In the rest of this book we shall look at different aspects of energies to give a basic awareness of subjects that we probably normally take for granted, thereby allowing us to make informed decisions and choices and thus extending our sense of responsibility for ourselves.

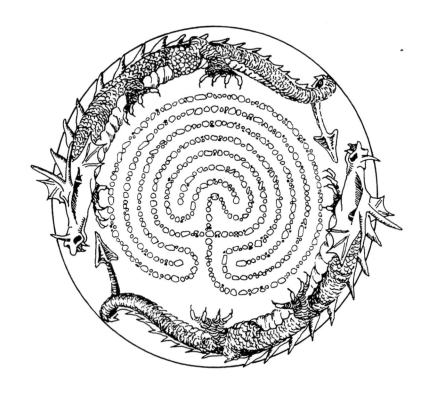

CHAPTER 2

EARTH ENERGIES

The earth is our home. This small blue planet "sited at the end of the 'unfashionable' western spiral arm of the galaxy", one of the planets circling the sun we call Sol, is home to humankind, as well as myriad other life forms, and is our very own portion of the universe.

Humanity's relationship to the earth appears to be a very recent thing in terms of the aeons the earth has existed. I say 'appears' because there are certain esoteric schools of thought that postulate that human consciousness itself has spent millennia dwelling in the myriad forms of existence on our planet since its 'birth'. There is an ancient Chinese saying which translates roughly as - 'Consciousness Sleeps in Minerals, Dreams in Plants, Dances in Animals and Awakes in Man!' Perhaps we are more intimately connected with our physical planet than we can ever imagine at this time.

To ancient cultures the earth was the Mother, whereas the Sky was the Father. The 'Mother' nurtured, provided and 'set the scene' - the archetypal creative act of the feminine Goddess energy. This Goddess energy was revered as Gaia, a living, breathing, being of great consciousness. The scientist, James Lovelock, with his theory of Gaia as a living organism well able to regulate her functions even without the help of humankind, touches upon this primeval concept of life given to us by the interaction of Mother/Father energies - the two becoming three.

As with the human body, the body of the earth is alive with energies. These energies, like the tides caused by the movement of the Moon, ebb and flow, pulsing across the landscape, intersecting here and there, creating vortexes of invisible forces that act on our consciousness and inner awareness.

Ancient people appeared to have had an innate sense of these energies and where these vortexes were perceived, or felt, monuments were placed, sometimes in the form of stone circles or mounds, making visible the invisible, for perhaps not everyone could 'see' these energies.

Plants, animals, birds and fish have always instinctively understood these energies which may possibly be magnetic or electrical in nature. Various cultures developed their own science, or art, of perceiving these energies. This art was known as Geomancy, which means 'divining the earth spirit'. Some of these energies may be positive or negative, or neutral in the electrical sense thus creating different areas of 'atmosphere'. This is not to say that the naturally negative areas are any worse for us than the positive or neutral areas, they are just different and certain types of animals, plants or people, may thrive in an area with one type of energy, whereas different plants, animals or people will thrive in a different location with different energies.

In the Western world in particular, humankind has become so separated from the natural world that we are in danger of becoming 'unnatural', or, at the least, just plain 'unwell'.

In the early 1900's, Alfred Watkins, author of 'The Old Straight Track', who had a great interest in legends concerning the landscape, discovered by a sudden insight, at the age of 70, that the landscape was criss-crossed with lines of energy that were marked on the land by holy places, churches, crossroads, trees, wells, mounds, standing stones and other sacred monuments. This web of lines, which were highly organised, stretched as far as the eye could see and there appeared to be distinct alignments which seemed to follow certain laws.

These lines, now commonly known as ley lines, have become a source of fascination for many people, and dowsers in particular, who with the aid of pendulums and dowsing rods, travel across the landscape tracking these lines of energy.

The Chinese, using their ancient geomantic art of Feng Shui, have a comprehensive understanding of the energies of the earth, although in their system, straight lines are not always harmonious and curves and meandering lines are considered auspicious.

The early Christian church recognised these energies and knew that certain sites had special or sacred energies and they built their churches on ancient places of power, thereby hoping to supplant the pagan deities. This is often depicted by the symbolism of slaying the dragon, which is possibly an analogy for the act of an upright pole, or spear, being stuck into the ground thus diverting, or redirecting, the energies of the earth in that area.

The symbols of pagan times were not immediately erased by the church and were often incorporated into the new buildings. Old churches abound with effigies of the Green Man and the stone was often intricately carved with the symbols of nature.

The symbol of the spiral was also used and has been found carved in stone and rocks all over Europe, in Russia, Egypt, India, and in Peru and Arizona in the new world. The Hopi Indians consider the design a symbol for Mother Earth.

The most sophisticated spiral was the labyrinth which is a precise and intricate pattern which has remained unchanged through thousands of years. The classical seven circuit labyrinth (see Chapter illustration), sometimes known as the Cretan design, is the form of single pathed magical maze that is most widely used around the world. Although it looks complicated, its method of construction is simple and is based on a cross, four right angles and four dots. Ancient labyrinths were often placed on power places, again possibly to mark invisible energies.

In Britain these labyrinths were often created in turf and were called Troy Towns, for the people of Northern Europe held Troy to be a key to the connection with the Mother Goddess energy at a time when patriarchy was gaining the upper hand, so in some way labyrinths were seen as a way back to the Goddess. There are also connections with the legend of Theseus and the Minotaur where the labyrinth appears to have become more of a maze which is a form of puzzle. The design of the classical labyrinth is, however, about fifteen thousand years older than the time of Theseus. In the early labyrinth myths it was always a woman in the centre, not a male monster as in the Greek legend.

There is also a connection with the Island of Delos and the Crane Dance, which is still danced today. The steps of this dance follow the path of the classical seven circuit labyrinth. The original crane dance was supposed to have been danced by Theseus, Ariadne, and those who fled with Theseus after the slaying of the monster. It was danced to celebrate their escape and was said to be the first time ever that men danced with women.

It is possible that many classical labyrinths developed into mazes when the Christian Church altered the design to incorporate a cross, thus quartering the circle and creating the need for choosing the right path.

Whilst labyrinths were placed on areas of power it is possible that it works both ways and that the creation of a labyrinth in a certain area alters the earth's energies in that area, in a beneficial way.

Ancient, and not so ancient, peoples also recognised the intangible effect of a place and sometimes personified this atmosphere which became the 'Genius Loci', the old Latin expression for the 'spirit of place'. The very word spirit can be taken to mean two different, but connected aspects. It can be the feel or sense of character of a place or exemplify a discarnate, supernatural being which has a distinct character and personality. It is possible that an early version of pilgrimage, and thus tourism, began in Roman times, and was developed by a recognition of the desire to encounter the Genius Loci of a place.

This sense of place appears to be lost or suppressed in our modern times and the dowser and consciousness researcher, John Steele, has referred to this loss as 'geomantic amnesia', where we no longer recognise that place has an effect upon our state of mind or well-being.

We also have the problem nowadays of being so constrained by the considerations of finance, work and space, that we appear to have very little choice over where we actually live. We cannot easily travel about the country, and expect to choose an exact location that feels just right for us, buy it and then decide exactly how and what we would build on that site. We usually have to compromise and most of us buy or rent a property that was sited and built any time over the last few hundred years.

However, it is still possible for us to discover what the feel or atmosphere is of the place we have chosen to make our home and to become aware of its energy and how it affects us. We could start by learning the history of the area, investigate the meaning of its name and whether there are any sites of interest such as monuments, standing stones, tumuli, wells, etc, nearby.

This affords us the opportunity to connect on an inner level with the 'spirit of place' and to develop a relationship with the land we live upon.

CHAPTER 3

RHYTHMS, CYCLES AND SYMBOLS

The eternal ebb and flow of human existence, the cycles of birth, life, death and rebirth, are all reflected in the annual cycles of the seasons and in the shorter cycles of months and days.

The earth turns once on its axis - that is called a day. If you are standing on one part of the earth, half of the time you face toward the sun and half of the time you face away from the sun.

Together this makes what we call a day. The ancient Maya called a day k'in and the Mayan word k'in also means Sun. This rhythm of light and dark has been called the Diurnal rhythm. A new name was given in 1960 by Franz Halberg of the University of Minnesota. This name was the Circadian Rhythm (meaning that which lasts about one day). Everything that lives responds in some way to this Circadian Rhythm, and many organic and chemical reactions are triggered by the effects of light and dark.

Living beings are also affected by the cycles of the moon. Originally the word month was 'moonth' and lunar rhythms were respected and understood in pagan and tribal societies.

The moon circles the earth once every 27.3 days, but the earth shows all of its 'faces' to the moon once every 24.8 hours. Because of gravitational effects the waters of the earth flow toward the moon and the tides are forty eight minutes later each day.

The definition of the Circadian Rhythm - about one day - allows the lunar rhythms to be included in the Circadian classification, however, the moon also produces another rhythm, which is the rhythm of the 'moonth'. Because the moon reflects light from the sun, the amount of moon we see depends on its position relative to the sun as well as to ourselves. Thus we get the divisions of the New Moon, Quarter Waxing Moon, Full Moon and Quarter Waning Moon. These traditional phases follow a cycle slightly longer than the lunar orbit - about 29.5 days from one Full Moon to the next. These 'moonths' were given names that reflected the ambience of the time of year, thus in British Pagan traditions we have the following poetic names:

> Snow Moon
> Death Moon
> Awakening Moon
> Grass Moon
> Planting Moon
> Rose Moon
> Lightning Moon

Harvest Moon
Hunters Moon
Falling Leaf Moon
Tree Moon
Long Night Moon
Ice Moon

As we are affected by cycles of light and dark we are also affected by the phases of the moon. Apart from the obvious connection with the feminine cycle of menstruation there are other cycles of behaviour connected with the moon phases. This may have something to do with the high water content in our bodies, but official organisations such as mental institutions and hospitals, as well as the police, notice increased erratic behaviour, and more accidents, at the time of the Full Moon.

The moon also appears to have an effect on the growth of plants and certain methods of farming and gardening, notably Bio-Dynamic farming, work with the phases of the moon to help the growth of crops. Again this may be connected with the water content of the soil and crops.

Over the centuries our calendars have undergone some revision. Since Julius Caesar decided to adopt the Solar Calendar in the year 45AD we have a system that follows the 365 and one quarter days per year cycle. However, this may not have been the most sensible calendar to adopt given that 365 is not an easily divisible number.

Robin Heath, in an article for Chalice Magazine (Issue 11 - Summer 1994), explains how the number 13 became unlucky, and how in fact 13 is the only sensible number to use when working out a calendar. The ancient calendar had 364 days and 364 is divisible by 13. Thereby we could have 13 months each of 28 days and each month would have four weeks of seven days, 52 weeks in each year and 13 weeks to each season. For this calendar to work with the solar rhythm we would have to have a leap year day in every year and two every four years. This concept was the 'year and a day' calendar of medieval times. So why did the number 13 become unlucky - it is obviously a very important number - a prime number - also important to the ancient Mayans. The Mayans used a perpetual 260-day sacred calendar called the Tzolkin. This sacred calendar has the ability the synchronise with a 24 hour cycle and with a whole range of other cycles. It is based upon a grid of 260 squares - 13 x 20 - giving a 260 day cycle. If you add a couple of zeros you have 26,000 - coincidentally 26,000 years is the approximate length of the zodiacal precession cycle, a major cosmic cycle.

The number 13 then is obviously a very special number, a sacred number, but was possibly considered to be too connected with pagan beliefs and had to be disempowered.

In 1801, Sir John Herschel discovered an 11 year sun spot cycle. This cycle has since been confirmed by many findings such as the thickness of annual rings in trees, the number of icebergs and the occurrence of drought and famine in India. All these events depend on the weather and it appears that this regular pattern of change in the weather is produced by the cycles of the sun. Computer analysis turned up another, longer, sun cycle - apparently the 11 year cycle peaks grow higher for about 40 years and then fade away to complete an 80-90 year cycle.

These links with the earth and her rhythms have been eroded through the centuries. The effect of the sun, moon and stars have been denigrated in our calendars and in our modern perceptions of popular astrology, a subject which has great depth and deep symbology. Many of us have also lost a connection with the stars in the sky at night. Street Lighting in towns and cities is certainly useful and appreciated, but has the effect of 'blotting out' the stars. There is something so evocative about star gazing on a clear, dark night. Something that stirs the deepest part of our being and makes us feel connected to the universe. Our ancestors saw patterns in the night sky that they related in some way to their lives. They also recognised the rhythms and cycles connected to the apparent movement of the stars and planets, thus developing the art of astronomy and astrology which were intimately linked in ancient cultures.

We have also lost our links with the fourfold and eightfold divisions of the year that were important in olden days. The importance of the Solstices and Equinoxes, the fire festivals of Imbolc, Beltane, Lammas and Samhain has diminished and we are poorer because of it. These festivals were an important celebratory event that brought communities together and gave them a sense of continuity, of connection with the earth and a sense of spiritual renewal. We would have felt part of everything, which would have been empowering, giving us a rightful sense of place and a connection with nature.

The Equinoxes mark the twice yearly event of the day and night being equal and occur on approximately 21st March and 21st September each year. The Solstices mark the longest day and the longest night of the year - Summer Solstice around the 21st June being the longest day and the Winter Solstice, around 21st December, being the longest night.

At the point of equal day and night in the Autumn, imagine the start of the next year's cycle. Nature's New Year's Day which signals an outpouring of energy on the invisible levels. Then at the Winter's Solstice imagine a great outbreathing, almost undetectable at first. The first snowdrop appears, the harbingers of Spring, followed by the outbursting of incredible energy into form - the Spring. The Spring Equinox is when the energy becomes action and we witness the miracle of rebirth.

The outbreath continues until the Summer Solstice when it reaches its furthest point. Then it pauses and we celebrate, with great joy, the sheer beauty and abundance of nature. And then the inbreath that gradually pulls inward whilst we celebrate the harvest of wheat, corn and fruit and the invisible levels of nature signal next year's cycle. The breath is gathered inward to its completion, and again, a pause, at the Winter's Solstice when we celebrate before the cycle begins again.

These are the rhythms our ancestors respected and acknowledged with the other four fire festivals of Imbolc, which celebrated the arrival of the ewes milk, Beltane celebrating the

24

arrival of the flowers, Lammas the harvest and Samhain, the gathering together of the stock to meet the winter.

The very act of celebrating a festival probably created an energy that sustained and renewed the land, the animals and plants, and the people, in a synergy of harmony and balance that attuned them to the creative forces that flowed through them and the land.

They would have also celebrated their own cycles and rhythms of birth, reaching maturity, marriage and death with appropriate ritual and ceremony, and would have connected themselves by the use of a symbolic language that goes deeper than any other form of communication.

A symbol is anything that represents or stands for something else, that implies things greater or other than itself. Carl Jung stated that a symbol is neither abstract nor concrete, neither rational nor irrational, neither real nor unreal. It is always both. He also said that as a plant produces its flower, so the psyche creates its symbols.

Symbols are frequently archetypal and could be considered as a pattern that in the physical dimension is a reflection of a pattern, or image, in non-material reality. The word archetype has its roots in the Greek words Arche, meaning beginning or origin and tupos (type) meaning image or pattern. So an Archetype is an original pattern, or beginning image.

Archetypes and symbols abound in all cultures and traditions, myths and legends, religions and organisations. Every aspect of our environment carries symbolic meaning and has an effect on us whether we are aware of them or not. These symbols may have a positive effect, such as making us feel relaxed, or a negative effect, causing us to feel apprehension, and where the 'real' and the 'symbolic' disagree, we often respond more strongly to the symbolic.

Some symbols are universal - geometrical shapes, representations of the sun, moon, stars, and constellations, etc, appear in most cultures throughout recorded history. Other symbols have meanings within a cultural group or society; the rainbow, for example, is very symbolic to the Aboriginal peoples, the rainbow representing the bridge between outer reality and the Dreamtime. The Ash Tree is very symbolic to the Norse people as it represent Yggdrasil, the World Tree. Indeed the imagery of the tree is a central symbol in many cosmologies as it represents nurture, the sustainer and the first and original home. In many cultures it represented the means to reach other levels of existence and in the Bible, the Tree of Knowledge held the fruit that gave the knowledge of good and evil.

The emblem used by the medical profession today is based on the ancient symbol of the Caduceus. The Caduceus was a staff entwined with two serpents, bearing two wings at the top, which was carried by Hermes (Mercury) as messenger of the gods. Also known as the Staff of Aesculapius, who was the Roman god of medicine or healing. Snakes, serpents and dragons were all revered by ancient cultures and had symbolic associations with wisdom, creation, the energy source of life, healing, fertility and treasure.

The ancient Caduceus symbolises the path of transformation and healing toward wholeness which is represented by evolution through the interaction of opposites spiralling into unity. It could also represent an unconscious awareness of the importance of the double helix spiral found in nature at the fundamental level of DNA.

Runes, Ogham Letters, Numbers and indeed Alphabets and Hieroglyphics are all symbolic representations of sounds and meanings. Some symbols are acquired by association or by similarities in appearance. The use of gold to represent the sun or silver the moon for instance. Then there are those symbols that are highly personal and have meaning within the family, or just for you personally.

One of the reasons why we like to buy something (virtually anything will do) from the place we spend our holidays, is because that object symbolises the concept of 'being on holiday in that particular place'. This is the whole idea behind souvenirs; they remind us of an experience, and objects that bring back pleasant memories may often become our personal symbols.

To the Greeks, the sacred centre of earth energy was called the Omphalos, meaning 'the navel of the world'. This was symbolically represented by a large stone, and the latter day foundation stones represent the Omphalos as well as the birth of a building.

For many centuries in the northern hemisphere, the potent symbol of the centre of the home was the hearth, with the symbol of fire at its heart. Indeed, if we look at the word hearth, we see it contains both the word heart and earth. It is our equivalent of the Omphalos - our centre. The hearth was the protector of life during cold winter months, provided the heat for cooking all meals and was the gathering place of the household where the family would share stories of times past, preserving family lore and educating the young.

Many modern homes today, with the advent of central heating, lack this symbol for the heart of the home - if anything, the focus in the room where the hearth would have been is the Television, almost symbolic of the All-Seeing eye, another ancient symbol.

As the hearth was considered the centre of the home, the walls represented the boundaries. In fact we cannot define the centre without a boundary around the edges. The boundary is the symbolic edge around our personal space and allows us to be in charge of what goes on in that space. We need boundaries that respond to the surroundings and the climate and we need to feel protected and nurtured, not trapped and isolated.

Depending on the religious aspirations of people, shrines and altars have sometimes been utilised to create a sacred centre in our homes. In many ways the mantlepiece of the traditional fireplace represented an altar, but once again many homes lack this connection. Not all of us follow a set religious path but we could perhaps bring the sense of the sacred into our lives and homes by using symbols that have meaning for us personally. Some people in the west are turning toward the eastern traditions to find this sacred or spiritual connection and they are creating spaces in their homes for meditation, contemplation, or just as a quiet retreat.

Personally I find it very satisfying to have around me crafts from different parts of the world as this symbolically represents to me a deeper connection to the whole earth and her people. A Japanese garden lantern, a Spanish waterfall, musical instruments from Africa, Arabia, South America and Australia, Tibetan Singing Bowls and a carved wooden Buddha that to me symbolises serenity, are all objects that I feel symbolise my connection with the greater whole. And this is the point, the symbols we use should make us feel more whole.

The large imposing buildings usually used by government organisations, schools, institutions, banks, etc, have long given us the message that we are powerless and make us feel diminished. At least in our own homes we can use and work with symbols that uplift and support us.

To strengthen our connection with the earth and the rhythms and cycles of nature, we can bring into our homes objects of nature. Plants can symbolise trees whereas stones can be symbolic of mountains and rocks. The Japanese have long used these symbols in their gardens to bring a spiritual dimension to their surroundings. They even use raked gravel to symbolise water.

At the time I write there is almost a mania for stars, moons and suns in interior decoration - on walls, ceilings, fabrics, lamps, candlesticks, etc, these motifs are appearing everywhere. If this is a fashion statement at least it seems to be more meaningful than most, as these symbols are powerful archetypes for all cultures.

Because the language of the unconscious mind is symbolic, whoever, or whatever, controls the symbols of a culture has the power which structures that culture's form. The media and the advertising industry are the master symbolisers of modern times as they try to sell by convincing us that unless we buy what they have to offer we cannot be happy, adult, sexy or fashionable.

We need to be aware of the power of symbols in our lives so we are in a position to select those which enrich and empower us. This is an area where we have choice as we have some control over what symbols we wish to have in our immediate surroundings.

In the following chapters we will be looking at shape and form, light and colour, sound and music, the use of plants and crystals, etc, and in some way all these things have a symbolic nature and they are all things that we can have some measure of control over.

We may not be able to move house, or start from scratch, but we can modify, alter and add to what we already have to enhance our lives and bring healing to our homes.

CHAPTER 4

SHAPE AND FORM

Shape and form mould our existence and give structure to the seeming chaos of thought, feeling and emotion, so the particular shape of form we choose to surround ourselves with, day in, day out, obviously has a great effect on us. It seems to be something we know little about and we take for granted the fact that in our western world we live in predominately rectangular homes.

Other societies have utilised many forms, the most familiar being the circular hut used by many tribal cultures, past and present. These tribal cultures are still very linked to the earth and her rhythms which are more cyclic than linear. These tribal societies did not always ignore the square, and in some cases it was incorporated into the circular structures such as the Native American Indian Medicine Lodges which often had four poles forming a cubic structure on the inside.

Squares and grids were used as a basis for layout by many cultures and societies when they became more 'civilised'. Many Hindu Temples and early Indian towns were laid out according to the Vastu-Purusha Mandala which is a square of squares, either eight by eight, or nine by nine. This grid of sixty-four or eighty-one squares exists in various forms from India to the West. Towns in Europe, including Britain, were often laid out on a gridwork pattern, but unlike the uncompromising grids of Manhattan, due consideration was given to the shape, contour and feel of the land, thus giving an almost organic feel to a perceived cosmic ideal.

Ancient cultures also used the combination of the square and circle as a basis for harmony and many Mandala patterns are based on the combination of these two archetypal shapes. It appears that through the reconciliation of the two shapes the essence of sacred architecture emerges, as the integration of the square and circle is a metaphor for equilibrium between heaven and earth.

I also feel that the square is linked to the left brain, which is the logical, reasoning and practical side, and that the circle is linked to the right brain, the intuitive, creative and visionary half of the brain. Because we are imbalanced at this time, favouring the logical left brain at the expense of the right brain, the square shape (and the double square, the rectangle) appears to dominate our society. We obviously need both the square and the circle to become whole and balanced.

It is interesting to note that in societies today where the people live simply in rugged and natural surroundings, their art and decoration often incorporates bold colours and strong geometric shapes with many straight lines. In many city environments, art and decoration show softer, more organic, curves. It appears we instinctively know that we need both strong lines and curves in our environment and we will compensate if one or the other is missing.

The site of the fourth century BC sanctuary of Asklepious, the healing god, at Epidaurus in Greece, was composed of square, circular and semi-circular buildings. Everyone who came to the temple for healing, regardless of their infirmity or wealth, had to walk the many kilometres from the port of Epidaurus to the Sanctuary. They then bathed in a sacred well and were possibly given herbs by the priests before sleeping there for the night. In the morning the dreams they had remembered were interpreted by the priests and became the basis for the healing. No-one was allowed to die within the Sanctuary (although I'm not sure how this was managed), and no babies were allowed to be born there, because birth and death were not allowed to happen within the Sanctuary.

Circles are a good shape to use to bring people together, a Meditation Sanctuary, a Village Community area, Discussion Area would all benefit from being enclosed within a circular space, but in our society we might not find them suitable for everyday living. Squares are very rigid as the 90 degree angles give abrupt changes in direction which could be considered stressful. It can, however, be a helpful shape if you feel the need to reorientate yourself if you have lost your bearings. When a square room has a flat ceiling it tends to feel like a box which is very deadening. Shaped ceilings can at least alleviate this problem a little.

Rectangles seem to be the shape that dominate our homes at this time possibly because our mechanically geometric thinking has established the convention of rectangular buildings, possibly a legacy from the order-orientated purpose of the Roman

Empire. Rectangular spaces have the best shape for storing objects in, and in our mechanistic view of reality what else are people but objects to be stored.

The architect, Christopher Day, in his book *Places of the Soul* cites a curious effect to a box-like rectangular room. When it is empty it is not in the least satisfying to our inner needs and we fill this need by filling our rooms. It is the objects that have to nourish us, even the most minimalist person needs some objects, as the room itself is not enough. In our present day consumerist society this is ideal as we just keep on buying objects to nurture our inner selves and to counter the deprivation that we feel in such shapes. If a room has interesting curves, shaped windows and doors and is generally softer in appearance than a box-like room, we find we are comfortable within that space without the need to stuff it full of possessions. Christopher Day points out that it is not the rectangle itself that is the problem but its 'life-sapping' characteristics.

There are some Architects, such as Christopher Day, who work with shape and form to create organic spaces that nourish us and make us feel whole.

Whereas we in Britain are generally unadventurous in the way we design our houses, there appears to be a greater awareness in other countries, particularly in Germanic countries and Scandinavia.

In these countries, a movement called the Baubiologie, or the Building Biology movement, is steadily growing. This system of architecture combines healthy building concepts with an ecological and spiritual awareness.

The founder of anthroposophy, Rudolph Steiner, also influenced the concept of organic architecture. In anthroposophic organic architecture a prime aspect is that form has a profound effect on behaviour and feelings, and consequently rectangular, and cubic, buildings cause people to act predominately in a rational, logical and materialistic way.

In America there also developed an organic architectural style, the most well known architect of this style being Frank Lloyd Wright, to whom organic design was the underlying inspiration and who once said:

Buildings, too, are the children of Earth and Sun.

Geometric principles underlie the forms found in living nature, but living forms do not have particularly straight lines. The use of angles, an ancient use in sacred architecture, is related to the cosmic world of geometric principles, more abstract than the organic world of living nature which builds on these geometric shapes to produce the infinite circular and spiralling forms.

The spiral is, of course, a very pertinent factor in organic matter. We have the double spiral that forms the helix of DNA, the spiral formation of shells and within the structure of many crystals, and it is possible that blood flows through the veins in a spiral motion. It has even been suggested that at the subatomic level, the circular motion of an electron about the nucleus of an atom is an illusion, and it is actually spiralling through matter and anti-matter. As we can only perceive it when it moves through matter, we see the illusion of a circular motion. All of this perhaps explains why it was of such symbolic importance to early peoples and why the labyrinth became so significant.

Wholly organic forms found in nature appear to lack the imprint of human consciousness which is not to say that they are without consciousness. The human state lies between the two extremes of the natural world and abstract concepts. Indeed the human body itself contains the proportions that were used in classical architecture, as does music and mathematics. These proportions are harmonious because they are inherent in all living forms as well as inanimate matter such as crystals and shells.

The basic measure that permeates all living matter is called the Golden Mean. The Golden Mean, or Phi, is the proportion of

1:1.6181 -

$$\frac{\sqrt{5} + 1}{2} = 1.6181:1$$

The spine and all natural things like plants, flowers and shells obey the rhythms and proportions of the Golden Mean and these proportions were central to Plato's and Pythagoras' numerological philosophy. It was used for the proportions of Egyptian and Greek temples, particularly for the Parthenon. Pythagoras claimed that the proportions of the Golden Mean were musical and the mathematician Filius Bonacci (Fibonacci) wrote a treatise on the number series related to the Golden Mean. This number series is known as the 'Fibonacci Sequence', where each number in the sequence is the sum of the two preceding number.

$$1 + 1 + 2 + 3 + 5 + 8 + 13 + 21 + 34 + 55 + 89$$

$$\frac{89}{55} = 1.6181$$

According to Helmholz, fundamental tones described by this series create pleasurable consonances in the brain. Kepler called it the 'divine proportion'.

Following on from the teachings of Pythagoras, Plato applied mathematics to explain the structure of the universe by using just three basic forms, the triangle, the square and the pentagon. By using these three forms and the ratios that generate them, he was able to show that these produced five regular solids, the platonic solids, which are the Tetrahedron, Octahedron, Hexahedron (Cube), Icosahedron and Pentagondodecahedron (see figure 1).

These five forms are the only possible forms in three-dimensional geometry that are bounded by plane surfaces having exactly the same shape and size. In each of these five forms, and in no other, the angles between the faces, and the

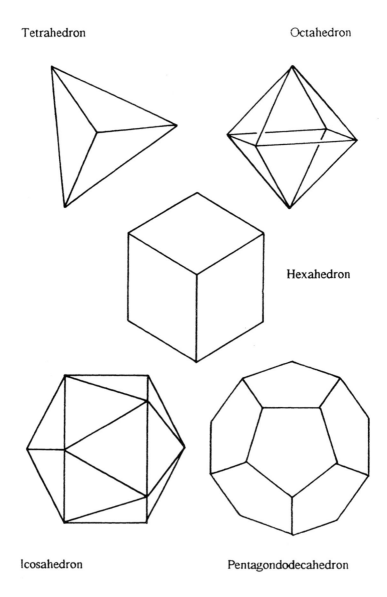

Tetrahedron

Octahedron

Hexahedron

Icosahedron

Pentagondodecahedron

Fig 1 Platonic Solids

angles between the edges, are the same, and the size and area of each of the faces is the same.

Each of the forms symbolically equate to the elements, the Tetrahedron to fire and the colour red, the Octahedron to air and the colour yellow, the Hexahedron to earth and the colour green, the Icosahedron to water and the colour blue, and the Pentagondodecahedron to ether and the colour violet. Ether is the esoteric substance said by mystics to permeate all space and contains the other four elements.

These geometric shapes underlie the forms found in the mineral, plant, animal and human worlds.

Two thousand years after Pythagoras, the great astronomer, Kepler, found that when these shapes were inscribed within spheres and within each other in sequence, the mathematics of the platonic solids described the orbits of the planets in the solar system.

The word 'geometry' itself literally translates as 'the measuring of the earth', and in his book *Sacred Geometry* (also published by Capall Bann), Nigel Pennick explains that geometry was the fundamental tool which underlies all that is made by the hands of people, geometry having developed from the earlier skill - the handling of measure, which in ancient times was considered to be magical. In those days magic, science and religion were inseparable.

One of my favourite Christmas presents as a child was a Spirograph and since that time I have been fascinated by the patterns that can be made by straight and curved lines, and by angles. In my book on Quartz crystal called *Crystal Clear*, I discuss the importance of angles, pointing out how closely related the word angles is to angels. One of this year's Christmas presents was the new book by David Pearson, called *Earth to Spirit - In Search of Natural Architecture*. In this book there is a quote by the Dutch Architect, Ton Alberts, which I was delighted to read:

Every angle has its own angel. There is ninety degrees
which has an angel. But between zero and ninety degrees
there are eighty-nine other degrees, so there are enormous
possibilities for calling all kinds of angels to come into our
buildings.

There is another figure used by ancient cultures which is called
the Vesica Piscis.

The Vesica (see figure 2) is created by two interpenetrating
circles, and where they overlap they form a pointed oval which
has been used for over two thousand years as a symbol for the
fish, thus Piscis. It is possible, by the use of the Vesica Piscis, to
work out geometric patterns without the use of a protractor as
from it can be derived the equilateral triangle. This figure
played a prominent part in the foundation of holy buildings and
is probably most well known as the symbolic design on the lid of
the Chalice Well in Glastonbury, designed by Frederick Bligh
Bond.

The ancient Egyptians studied, and had a great understanding
of shape and form. The most well known structure, of course,
being the great Pyramid of Cheops. The pyramid, regardless of
its original purpose, has interesting properties which are still
being researched. The ability of this shape to sharpen razor
blades or to preserve dehydrated food within its structure
obviously gives us a clue that shape affects the things inside it.
I suspect that pyramids were never intended to be lived in, but
can be used to effect, particularly in relation to meditation and
healing, as it appears to have a somewhat 'mind-blowing' and
'time-removing' energy. This could be because shape and form
are very important to the way energy flows. The energy that
flows upward from the earth appears to be stronger around
corners and sharp edges. It also flows along and around certain
shapes and generally shapes with a peak have strong and
positive energies within them. It has also been suggested that
domes close off a space both aurally, visually and magnetically.

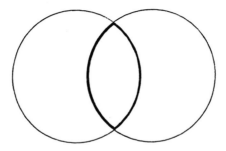

Fig 2 Vesica Piscis

The use of the rectangle and square without its counterpart, the circle, has resulted in spaces which seem to have the effect of dulling our perceptions. The Colour Therapist, Theo Gimbel, who has extensively researched the subjects of form, sound, light and colour, has suggested that the use of the Icosahedron shape could give an effect that is too spacy and aimless and that a Tetrahedron would stifle us. The Pentagondodecahedron, with artistic modifications is the shape most recommended for pure living space and healing spaces. For most of us this is very impractical, however, he has come up with a simple re-design which mitigates the 90 degree angle which is so much overused today. He calls this a 'triangular conversion' (see figure 3). This has the effect of transmuting the 'hardness and squareness' of 90 degree corner angles.

An alternative would be to use corner furniture or even build an internal curve across the corner to soften its effect.

It may be possible that hexagonal or octagonal shapes may be beneficial, certainly the Chinese have held the Octagon to be a very auspicious shape. It appears that rooms with irregular multi-angled walls cause unease, but regular multi-angles walls, as with the Octagon, seem to be advantageous.

Most of us, however, find ourselves living in homes with square or rectangular rooms with flat, unrelenting ceilings that are at best just plain uninteresting, and at worst, oppressive and deadening. Shaped ceilings, domes, arches, pitched roofs, conical shapes and vaulted ceilings would completely change the character of the blandest room. There is not much you can do with these flat ceilings although it is possible in some rooms to alter the effect of the ceiling by using material to form an internal tent-like structure. Pale colours will lessen their oppressive effect, but with a fairly high ceiling you might prefer a darker shade to help define the boundary of the room. You could also add interest by hanging things from the ceiling.

The shape of windows and doors can also alter the energy of a room. Again, for convenience, most windows and doors these

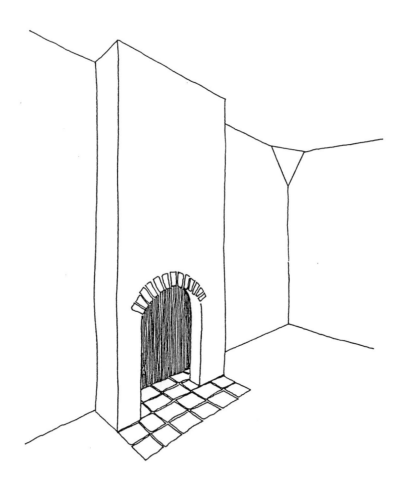

Fig 3 Triangular Conversion

days are composed of straight lines. Arched windows and doors give interest and are aesthetic and appealing. Circular windows give a somewhat oriental flavour (they are known as Moon windows in the East) and the arched shape of the gothic window, gives a room a sense of drama.

As we do not usually consider the effect shape and form have on our sense of well-being, it would be sensible for further research to be carried out on this subject.

As individuals we may only be able to make minor adjustments to the shape of our rooms, however, if we at least recognise that shape and form have an impact on our lives, this would be a worthwhile start.

CHAPTER 5

LIGHT AND COLOUR

All living things have evolved over the aeons of history under the light of the sun and the rhythm of alternate light and dark.

Almost all the myths of creation involve darkness and light. The seeds of creation are cultivated in the womb of darkness to be born into the light and into revelation. Darkness contains the potential, that which is unknown, and this is why it has been universally feared. It has strong links with the unconscious mind, with the world of sleep and dreams and despite our fears we need the dark as much as we need the light.

Light and dark are potent symbols that act on our minds as well as having tangible effects on our physical bodies. Light symbolises warmth, activity, creativity, intuition (seeing the light), goodness, holiness, revelation and spiritual progress, whilst darkness can represent unknown fears, coldness and inactivity. Yet psychologically we need both light and dark and all they represent. We need our time of activity and our time of rest and renewal. As natures rests in the darkness of the earth each winter, so we rest in the darkness of each night and are renewed and refreshed each morning.

Our biological clocks are attuned to the rhythms of light and dark and hormone patterns respond to the levels of increasing or decreasing light during the seasons. There is even a medically recognised disorder known as "Seasonal Affective Disorder" - SAD, which affects people susceptible to the falling levels of light during the winter which is characterised by depression, fatigue, weight gain and carbohydrate craving. The treatment for this condition consists of exposure to bright full spectrum artificial lighting which is five times brighter than normal room lighting.

The therapeutic value of sunlight has been recognised for many thousands of years. The Babylonians, Egyptians, Greeks and Romans all practised sun bathing for health reasons and it appears that light is the most important factor in our health after water and food.

Light is perceived by our eyes but is also absorbed directly through our skin and may even reach the brain through the skull. Sunlight contains a balanced distribution of the visible wavelengths of light including ultraviolet and the short wave infrared. Ultraviolet light is of vital importance to our physical well-being as it has been found to stimulate blood circulation and the glands, lessen fatigue and helps to increase the release of endorphins and assist in the production of Vitamin D. Its

44

negative effects appear due to overexposure, or sudden exposure to a stronger sun than we are used to, such as a Mediterranean holiday two weeks out of fifty-two. Sunburn, wrinkled skin, cataracts and the risk of skin cancer are all avoidable with sensible precautions.

Natural light is variable and subtly changes during the course of the day. Early morning and late evening sunlight is red-orange and is low in intensity whilst the light at noon is of high intensity and is bluish. This light may be diffused by clouds or be dappled by the leaves of the trees and the interplay of light and shade gives interest and keeps us stimulated and alert.

Natural light indoors is also varied. It may be direct, shining straight through a window and may cast shadows and cause glare. Reflected light is bounced off surfaces, either outside or inside the room and depending upon the texture or brightness of the surfaces the light may be muted or tinted with colour. Light that passes through frosted glass, net curtains or blinds is filtered and becomes soft and diffuse.

Particular tasks in different rooms need direct light and lighting for the kitchen, office/study, workroom and stairs, needs to be bright. The rooms that are used for relaxation and comfort require a more diffused and reflected form of lighting which is as variable as the effect of dappled sunlight.

In an ideal world we would all have access to natural daylight. The ancient South American Indian cultures recognised the vital importance of light to well-being and had 'sun rights' where neighbours were not allowed to build where it would infringe on the availability of sunlight.

If it were possible we would also benefit from connecting ourselves to the cycle of the sun and the four directions by awakening with the light of the morning sun from the east, carrying out our daily activities in the south light (except in hot climates), relaxing in the west light and retreating when required to the northern light.

John D. Ott, the photographer who filmed the beautiful time lapse nature sequences for Disney, studied the effect of light and colour for many years and as a consequence of this research he developed glass that allowed the full spectrum of daylight (including a small amount of ultra-violet) to shine through. This glass, known as Full Spectrum Glass has been used with great success in offices, schools and homes in America. He also developed full spectrum lenses for spectacle wearers which allow the full spectrum of natural daylight to reach the eyes.

Ideally we need to bring as much natural light into the home as possible, but we are often constrained by the positioning and the number of windows and have to rely on some form of artificial light which, of course, we require when the sun goes down.

Artificial lighting needs to be chosen with care. Good lighting and its position should help avoid any health problems such as headaches and eyestrain and should also contribute to the mood and atmosphere of our homes. Most of us in the western world use electricity to produce light and the most commonly used lights are incandescent lamps (ordinary light bulbs), and fluorescent lighting. Incandescent lamps are heavily weighted toward the red end of the spectrum and have little blue or green light. This is why these lamps give a yellow cast to the room. This at least is more in keeping with the morning and evening effect of natural daylight.

Fluorescent lighting does the reverse, it has more blue and green and less red and yellow, although you can buy 'warm whites' which help offset the "cold" effect of fluorescent light. Ordinary fluorescent lighting is not particularly beneficial to the human system, and the flicker effect it produces can also aggravate certain conditions such as epilepsy.

This form of lighting was developed just before World War II and was only supposed to be used during the war as emergency lighting. The inventor had apparently stipulated that it should not be used as ordinary lighting on a full time basis as he felt it could possibly be detrimental to health, however, since it proved to be very cheap it has continued to be used in homes, offices, schools and factories, etc.

Full Spectrum lighting has now been developed which offsets the negative effect of fluorescent lighting and gives a near approximation of natural daylight including small amounts of the ultraviolet wavelength.

These products cannot be advertised in the US as health products and in some cases there has been concern over the levels of Ultraviolet radiation. Apparently, if these lights are over-used there may be a problem in some areas because of the increased levels of Ultraviolet reacting with hydrocarbon pollutants in the air, which may create a photo-chemical smog. Flicker-free converters have also been added to these lamps to offset the flicker effect that can be so detrimental, the only problem being, of course, the extra expense involved in purchasing such lighting.

The more modern types of fluorescent tubes have been designed to accelerate the cycle which produces the flickering and to reduce the associated hum produced by the tubes, but it is not certain yet whether these are effective. All fluorescent tubes emit higher electromagnetic fields (EMF's) than other light sources, which may have a detrimental effect on some people.

The lighting design itself should be as natural looking as possible and light fittings should be placed where not too many of the fittings themselves are visible. Bright light sources and naked bulbs need to be shaded or they become stressful focal points. The only valid way to create an appropriate atmosphere as well as good lighting is to experiment as there are no real hard and fast rules as all situations vary.

The new generation of lamps are energy efficient and although they have a higher initial purchase price, their long life and efficiency make them a cheaper option in the long run.

Whatever lighting we choose for our homes we must not forget the old fashioned candle. The use of candles in this country is becoming more and more popular. Candlelight is gentle, romantic and creates a meditative and contemplative atmosphere that gives a healing ambience to any room. Candles, however, require constant supervision. The effect of firelight is also uplifting and healing, but of course many homes do not even have a fireplace. Candles, although only a tiny flame, can bring the presence of the spirits of fire and light into your home and remind you of the mystery and magic of life. Just one candle burning in the dark is a potent symbol that helps us to connect with something greater than ourselves.

Darkness and light, where the two meet we find colour, the child of light and dark. Colour is everywhere and is part of everything and yet it is an illusion created by the vibrational frequencies of a very small part of the electro-magnetic energies. Colour can uplift or depress, stimulate or soothe, provoke or inhibit. It works on conscious and unconscious levels having symbolic, psychological and physical effects. It has been shown that colour has an effect on people even if they are blind or colour blind, so even if we fail to notice the colours around us they are still influencing us.

The spectrum of visible light contains all colours and each colour it its own right offers us its particular frequency which we can utilise for our well-being.

When we decorate with colours we are also working with light as the colour schemes of walls ceilings, floors and furnishings can absorb, reflect or transmit the light in their vicinity. It therefore follows that every situation has to be assessed individually taking into account the amount and type of light available both naturally and artificially, the size and shape of the room or area involved, and the texture of the surfaces.

As colour can be such a powerful influence on our homes, and ourselves, we shall look carefully at how we can make use of it. There are two aspects to the use of colour in the home. The first is the design aspect, the way colours work in relation to each other and their characteristics. The second aspect is the application of colour in relation to the symbolic, psychological and physical influences - in other words - setting the mood for the appropriate uses of the room and to give us the most optimum and healing benefit.

Let us start by looking at the attributes of colour. Colour can do all sorts of tricks - it can emphasise form, for example, a dark piece of furniture would stand out well against a white background wall. It can create movement - bright spots of colour around a room tend to make your eye move from one brilliant accent to another. It can open up walls or close them in, imagine the difference between a room painted light blue and the same room painted dark brown. Dark colours absorb more light than light colours and this also needs to be taken into account when selecting finishes.

When planning colour schemes it is important to work with the three qualities of a colour which are Hue, Light Value and Chroma, or Intensity. These three dimensions produce a 'solid' of colour (see figure 4). The Hue is the chromatic colour, ie, Red or Blue. The Light Value determines whether a colour is pale or dark depending on the amount of light which it can reflect. At the top of the scale we have white and at the bottom we have black.

The Chroma or intensity is the brightness or dullness of a hue, its strength or its weakness. A strong colour has full chroma, a weak or soft colour is nearly neutral grey.

Normal colour is the middle value between light and dark on the Value Chart. Values lighter than the normal colour are called tints and usually have white added. Shades are values darker than the normal colour and usually have black added.

If only the Hue is considered the result would be colourful but lacking in subtlety. If only the Light Value is considered you would get a somewhat monochromatic scheme full of variations

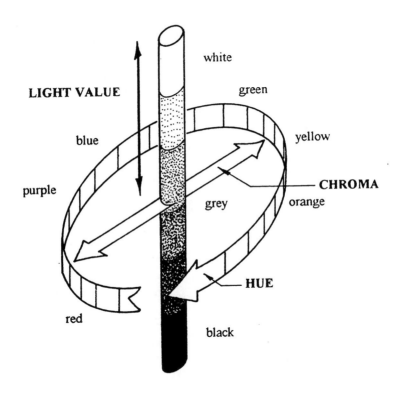

Fig 4 Solid of Colour

of tints and shades but lacking in contrast and vitality. If only the Chroma, or intensity, is considered you may get variety in colour sensation but there may be an absence of light and shade.

To avoid these difficulties, make sure that the colours you choose do not have the same tone and intensity. For example, if you decided to take the three primary colours of red, yellow and blue, then a full intensity yellow (full Chroma) with a pale blue (light and a little Chroma), and a dark soft red (dark and low Chroma), could make an interesting and subtle scheme.

To understand how designers use colour we need to look at the Colour Wheel (see figure 5). In this colour wheel I have used eight colours, the seven colours of the rainbow plus Magenta, a wonderful rich lilac pink which is created when you bring together red and violet. It could be considered as the first colour of the next octave, being a 'finer version' of the colour red.

When we create a colour wheel in this way we are visually able to show the complementary colours. These are the colours that are diametrically opposite each other on the wheel. When blended together as pigments the two colours would create grey. However, if we used coloured light and blended them together, the two colours would create white light.

The complementary colour is the colour the eye adjusts to after being saturated in any one colour for more than 15-20 seconds. This effect can be noted by looking at, for example, the colour green for 20 seconds or so, then by looking at a white background. The complementary colour will be observed for about the same amount of time, in this instance the complementary colour is magenta. This effect is called an after-image.

Any subtle variation in one colour correspondingly changes the complementary colour. For example, if you looked at a 'bluer' green, then the after-image would be a 'redder' pink.

The colour wheel also groups warm colours together, ie yellow, orange and red, and the cool colours together, ie violet, blue and turquoise - the two groups being separated by a 'neutral' colour - green and magenta.

Once the identity of the colours has been established in this way, it is easier to see that those colours tending to lean towards each other will harmonise, whilst those that lean away will clash, for example, a bluish red will go with a reddish blue, whereas a yellowish red will not harmonise so well.

Clashes are more obvious at the red end of the spectrum but they can be used together when the chroma and light values are varied. If they are used together at full intensity we may find them psychologically disturbing.

Bear in mind that the colour of the largest area of the room determines the scheme, or key, to the room composition. To consider which colours work well together we can work with several options on the Colour Wheel (See Figure 6).

A Monochromatic scheme is based on one hue only and uses tints and shades. This can be considered safe but possibly dull and it relies on a good use of texture and form to create further interest. However, these schemes can be very pleasing and restful, although it will create a situation where one psychological quality will dominate.

An Apposite scheme is based on two closely related or adjoining Hues. Interest can be created by using different Light Values and intensities, but again this is usually a quiet scheme.

A Complementary Scheme is where two diametrically opposite, or near opposite, Hues are used, such as blue and orange. Again this scheme needs to use a variation of Light Value and intensity. This creates a more visually interesting scheme and does tend to balance psychological qualities.

The Colour Wheel

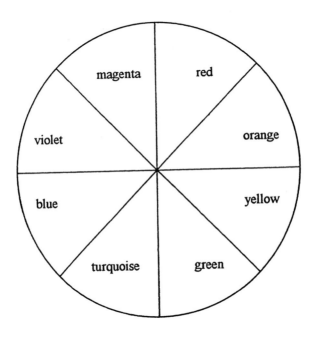

Fig 5 Colour Wheel

A Triadic Scheme is based on three colours that are spaced at approximately one third intervals, for example, violet, green, and orange. This is a well-balanced but bold scheme as you have to use three colours that would clash at full intensity. However, by varying Light Value and intensity this could be achieved.

A Split-Complementary Scheme is a three-way division using two colours adjoining, or close together and one colour that is opposite, for example, orange, yellow and blue. This usually creates a successful scheme.

A Double Split-Complementary uses two adjacent colours and two opposite adjacent colours - yellow and green with violet and magenta, for example. This is quite an ambitious scheme but is full of vitality and interest.

Different colours have differing characteristics which are noted below.

Red, orange and yellow are warm, advancing colours. They attract the eye because their energy seems to move toward us. They are called magnetic colours. They are best used as highlight colours at full intensity as they tend to appear more prominent. They can be used very successfully in their pastel tints in large quantities.

Yellow, however, can be used successfully at full intensity as it is the colour that reflects the most light.

Turquoise, blue and violet are cool, receding colours. Their energy is expansive and appears to move away from us. They are called electrical colours and are very good background colours.

Depth is created by using receding colours in the background and advancing colours in the foreground.

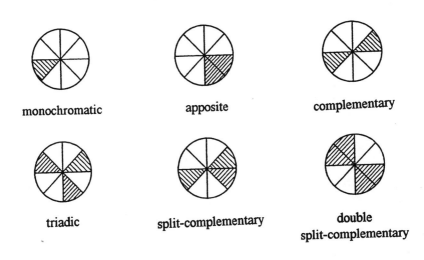

monochromatic   apposite   complementary

triadic   split-complementary   double
                                              split-complementary

Fig 6 Options on the Colour Wheel

Red, orange and yellow are more likely to irritate than green, turquoise, blue, violet or magenta.

Poor colour schemes in dress and the environment can lead to fatigue and the eye can be shocked by colours if they are too intense.

Rough surfaces tend to dull intensity through absorption. Smooth surfaces which reflect more light rays increase colour intensity.

Simultaneous contrast is the tendency of a colour to throw its complementary into surrounding areas.

If two complementary pigment colours of the same intensity are placed together, each will intensify the other. If we place magenta and green together, the magenta intensifies the green and the green intensifies the magenta. The result will be that each colour will compete for attention with equal force, resulting in a dancing or vibrating effect along the edge where the two colours meet. To overcome this effect we can lower the intensity of one of the colours or separate them by the use of black, white or grey.

A contrast of colours is used where variety, excitement or the emphasising of important detail is desired. Contrast should be avoided when calm, peace and receding colour effects are needed.

The background behind a particular colour can change the apparent hue of a colour. A colour can appear more intense and bright by surrounding it with a neutral grey. All colours look brighter against a black background. Colours appear darker on a light background.

The best light source when matching colours is natural daylight. Direct sunlight can produce too much glare. However, you will need to bear in mind that the type of artificial lighting you are using will have a different effect on various textures and surfaces. Always check the match if possible under the type of light you will be using.

Always let a colour dry before checking a colour match - pigments look different wet than they do when dry.

We will now look at the symbolic, psychological and physical effects of colour and how it affects our moods and emotions. Please note that the details on the physical effects are for interest only. To use colour as a physical therapy you would need to consult a fully trained colour therapist, and, in all cases of ill-health it is advisable to seek proper medical attention.

Colour in the form of pigment has less effect than coloured light on the body, however, it is useful and interesting to know its physical properties.

Both the positive and negative psychological effects are given - too much of any one colour can tend towards the more negative effect.

We are all aware that we use colour terms in our language - usually to indicate emotional effects such as "seeing red", being "green with envy", having the "blues", being "in the pink", and "seeing the world through rose-tinted glasses". We speak of someone who shows very little emotion as being colourless and we speak of people's views and opinions being coloured.

Some of these effects are due to cultural conditioning and can vary from culture to culture as they are using a symbolic language - however, there does seem to be a correlation between colour and emotion at a deep level of our being that is worthy of our interest.

Let us look at each colour in turn.

RED

The colour red has the longest wavelength and the lowest, densest energy of visible light. It is thought to be the first colour perceived by babies, or by anyone who has been unexposed to light for a long time. It is the fastest moving colour in terms of catching the eye and has the greatest impact.

It is a stimulating colour - dominant, forthright, takes command, loves authority, can be bossy, shows strength of will and courage. It represents physical love, new life, new beginnings, activation, warmth, goodwill and prosperity. It is outgoing, aggressive, impulsive, vigorous, ambitious, optimistic and restless.

Its negative qualities are rage, anger, hate and brutality, or a sense of sin and shame, particularly in sexual terms.

It has a stimulating and invigorating effect on the physical body and tests have shown that the heart rate increases, blood pressure may rise and breathing may become shallower if we are surrounded by a red environment. It is useful to help the circulation and to stimulate the nervous and muscular systems. It increases vitality and is helpful in alleviating anaemia and hypothermia.

It is inadvisable to use red for someone whose system has an over-abundance of red to begin with, or in cases of heart problems.

Because of its stimulating and activating qualities it is a good colour to decorate gyms, playrooms, morning rooms, indeed any room where there may be physical activity.

It is good for parties and dancing, but despite its sexual connotations, it is not a good colour to use in the bedroom. If you wish to make use of its stimulating effects use a red light which you can switch off! It is not advisable to use a strong red in the Dining Room because being surrounded by red at every meal may make the digestion suffer as this colour causes fermentation. It is used commercially in restaurants as it does give a cosy effect and stimulates the appetite in the short term. It also has the effect of slowing down time so you would tend to finish the meal quicker under a red influence and would be surprised at how little time had elapsed.

Red is ideal as an accent colour - the odd splash of red here and there to catch the eye and create movement. To cover a large area it may either be darkened to maroon or burgundy, or lightened to shades of pink.

Red walls would appear to reduce space and also create a sense of drama. Red also increases the apparent size and importance of objects.

Its complementary colour is turquoise blue.

ORANGE

This colour has been referred to as "The Kiss of Life". It is the colour of health and vitality. Orange is the warm 'warmth' colour - red can stray to cooler blue mixtures and yellow to cooler greens, but orange is always warm.

Orange is an earth colour associated with autumn. It is wholesome and homely. It can have exotic overtones, reminiscent of spices and saffron robes.

It inspires confidence, encourages ambition and brings out creative qualities and the use of the imagination. It is cheerful, optimistic, companionable and sociable. It helps to expand the horizons of the mind. It is the colour of bliss and joy, full of enthusiasm, spontaneous, jovial, flamboyant and good-natured.

Its negative qualities are folly, empty foolish chatter, conceit with an inflated ego, exhibitionism and destructiveness.

In the physical body it stimulates the metabolic rate, aids in cases of asthma, alleviates indigestion disorders, alleviates cramps and spasms and has a generally cleansing effect on the system.

Because of its sociable qualities orange is excellent to use in rooms where conversation is to be encouraged, and it is good for parties and for rooms where groups gather together. Pubs often use orange lighting in small doses which encourages conversation and sociability.

It is a very welcoming colour so is ideal for hallways. It is suitable in Dining Rooms if balanced by its complementary as it aids the digestive system.

In its full intensity it would not be very good for the bedroom, study or office as it would tend to stimulate too much conversation.

Again it is a colour that at full chroma would be ideal as a highlight but would need to be used as a pastel - all the lovely tints of peach and apricot, or deepened to burnt orange, ochre, terracotta and all the lovely autumn shades, to use in any quantity.

Remember too that brown is really a very dark orange and in this darker form becomes quite restful. This colour is particularly good in rooms with a cool (north or east facing) aspect to add warmth, but would need to be offset with a pale warm tint to give light.

Its complementary colour is blue.

YELLOW

Yellow is always a comparatively light colour, for when it ceases to be light it ceases to seem yellow. Thus it is a natural symbol for enlightenment.

It is, however, conspicuously lacking in popularity, although it is very popular with the Chinese. In ancient China it was a colour worn only by the Emperor "the Son of Heaven".

Yellow increases self control, opens the intellect and activates wisdom. It is the colour of joy and cheerfulness.

It stimulates intelligence, brain logic and imagination, ingenuity, decisiveness, discernment, optimism, a sense of reason, philosophy and shrewdness.

Its negative qualities indicate rigidness of thought, flattery, exaggeration, malice, vindictiveness, craftiness and cowardliness.

Its effect on the physical body is cleansing and purifying. It acts on the spleen, pancreas, liver and kidneys. It aids digestion and clears sluggish conditions. It increases the flow of vital fluids in the body and has beneficial effect on the nervous system. It helps to alleviate constipation, worms, piles, deafness, arthritis and rheumatism. It also stimulates the lymph system.

It is a colour that needs to be used wisely as a too yellow environment can be disorientating and can lead to a loss of mental balance. This can then lead to violence. However, when used with plenty of white it is a cheerful, sunny colour that is particularly good for kitchens and breakfast rooms. It goes very well with green for a fresh country feel. As a sunny colour it would be good for rooms that receive very little sunlight.

It is a colour that can be used successfully at full intensity in reasonable quantity provided it is offset with other colours. Lemon tints are very accommodating and go very well with greens and blues. Gold is also very easy to use and to live with. However, avoid using gold and lemon together and watch for changes of colour under artificial light.

Yellow's complementary colour is violet.

GREEN

Green is associated with balance and harmony. It is the colour of the planet Venus and is therefore associated with love - it also symbolises fertility.

Green is the most restful colour for the eyes as the lens of the eye focuses green light almost exactly on the retina. Theatres have a Green Room so that the players may rest their eyes (and nerves) after the glare of the stage lights.

It is the colour of growth and hope, of evolution, equilibrium, harmony, knowledge and faith and gives a feeling of freedom and space. It relaxes the emotions as it has a neutral quality, and helps to calm the nerves and relieve anxiety.

It gives self control and helps one feel centred, symbolises justice, and is the colour associated with sympathy, understanding, humour, adaptability and conscientiousness. It is also associated with prosperity and abundance.

Its negative qualities are envy, suspicion, deceit, lack of judgement, callousness, grievance, injustice, treachery and dishonesty.

In the physical body it is the great harmoniser and balancer. It aids muscle and tissue building and helps against colds and influenza and is good for alleviating headaches, particularly those caused by eyestrain. It can help control blood pressure, is useful for alleviating hayfever, neuralgia, billiousness, malaria and the effects of shock.

Green also needs to be used wisely in decoration. As we have so much green in nature, which is a living green, it does not always translate so well into pigments. It is a restful colour but if overdone can create a situation where you feel drained of energy. However, if used with other colours it is a delightful colour to use in all its tints and shades. It is particularly pleasing with magenta, and all shades of pink. It goes well with yellow, blue and peach, and indeed it has an adaptability that allows it to go well with all the other colours. One of the best ways to use green in any room is in the form of living plants which are an ideal accessory to any colour scheme.

Remember that if you plan to use deep green textiles, make sure they don't appear black under artificial light.

Green can be used in any room but is not so good for active areas. It can be used fairly extensively in its paler tints. Jade and emerald are fairly lively versions and lime green is a very stimulating and exciting colour. Traditional interiors look well in Celadon (grey-green), Wedgewood, Forest Greens and Olive.

Green's complementary colour is magenta.

TURQUOISE

The colour of the sky and sea on a summer's day, turquoise is rapidly becoming a very popular colour and has been very popular in Turkey for centuries, in fact it is their national colour.

Turquoise is the colour of clarity and communication and is a great aid to all who teach or give lectures. It is self-sufficient and has an inner resistance.

It is the first colour to bring through the more spiritual qualities and gives spiritual as well as mental and emotional clarity. It aids the transformation process and promotes a change in consciousness. It is discriminating, poised and sensitive.

Its astringent quality is a great aid to relieve itching and stings and it is especially good for skin problems. It is useful to alleviate inflammatory conditions, burns, bruises and swellings. It aids the immune system and is good for throat problems.

Because of its relaxing, yet refreshing, qualities it is an ideal colour for many rooms - Sitting Rooms, Offices, Bedrooms and

Bathrooms, particularly as it is one of the most flattering colours for the western complexion.

It is expansive and would make a room appear larger and lighter. To add warmth use with red or pink but it also goes well with peachy tints. Mixed with a touch of green it turns into a beautiful aqua that is very accommodating.

Turquoise's complementary colour is red.

BLUE

Blue is the peacemaker of colours. It is soothing and soporific and stands for truth, trust and security.

It is the colour of spirituality and promotes contentment, is faithful and constant, indicates refinement, beauty and serenity. Blue gives us aspiration and faith, contemplation, peace and tranquillity, devotion, loyalty, reliability, stability, resourcefulness, tactfulness, patience and steadfastness .

In its negative state it is over-ambitious, suspicious, distrustful, unfaithful and lazy. If overdone it leads to a feeling known as "the blues" - a melancholy state of mind.

In the physical body it lowers blood pressure and the pulse-rate. It promotes deeper exhalation, induces sleep, and is antiseptic and astringent. It reduces inflammation, alleviates headaches, migraines, thyroid disorders, throat problems and children's ailments, sun or heatstroke.

It is a very popular colour in all its variations but is one of the most difficult colours to match successfully. It is non-threatening and is therefore a good colour to use in dentist's and doctor's waiting rooms.

It enlarges space and is very good for bedrooms as it helps to promote sleep. It does need accents and highlights of a warm colour otherwise it can be decidedly chilly. It works well with orange, yellow, green and pinky reds.

Pale blues can be difficult to use as they are the tones most likely to appear cold, but they can be put with lilac, pale green or white for a delicate effect and with browns and peaches to add warmth. The darker blues of navy and indigo are heavy and dramatic and would need to be offset with paler tones.

Blue is an excellent colour to use in offices where there is a lot of activity to counteract stress and tension. Good also for use in treatment rooms and healing areas.

Blue's complementary is orange.

VIOLET

The red and blue of which violet is composed are physically, emotionally and symbolically poles apart. Since the mind may be confused as to whether it is responding to the masculine red, or the feminine, spiritual, blue, the various shades of violet are defined as 'psychologically oscillating'. They are colours about which people feel either delight or aversion.

Violet promotes self-esteem, it inspires, is artistic and psychic. It indicates idealism, self-sacrifice, serenity, tranquillity, poise and humility. It has a quality of luxury and can be very sensual. It gives intuition, integration, practical idealism, clarity and perception, fluency, articulation, co-ordination, and a sense of unity. It also gives a sense of occasion and is associated with ceremony, ritual and dignity, often seen as a royal colour that has been restricted in the past to certain spiritual ranks, it does not even today seem quite appropriate for everyday use.

Its negative qualities are superstition, idolatry, contradiction, impracticality, intolerance and disintegration.

On the physical level it acts on the pituitary gland and helps nervous disorders and mental problems and alleviates excessive emotional disturbance. It can be particularly useful in cases of mental obsession. It helps alleviate eye, ear and nose problems, scalp and hair disorders, catarrh and sinus congestion and generally purifies.

In its darker shades of purple and plum it is a very heavy and forceful colour. Research on colour and perceived noise has shown that white rooms sound the loudest whilst the quietest colour for a room is purple. Full of dignity and slightly mournful, these shades are ideal for Halls of Remembrance and Churches, but would need to be used with care in the home.

The lighter shades of lavender and mauve are very pleasing and are good bedrooms colours. These colours would be enlarging and receding and would make rooms appear larger. They look wonderful with magenta and pinks, go well with green and blue and are offset by yellows.

Violet inspires contemplation and would be very useful in a room used for meditation. It is a slightly 'other worldly' colour, full of fantasy and is very good for creative and artistic people or for those who have overtaxed their reasoning minds.

It does however have one quality that needs watching for. It is exceedingly expansive and needs careful handling to avoid it taking over your colour scheme (or your wardrobe!).

Violet's complementary is yellow.

MAGENTA

So named because the colour was 'discovered' as a pigment in the year of the Battle of Magenta, in Italy, in 1859.

Magenta represents love - spiritual love and universal friendship, gentleness, tenderness and sympathy. It has a sense of divinity and has great compassion. It gives balance, reverence, dedication, artistry, realisation and actualisation. It helps us to let go when troubled and has a great sense of unity and brings people together.

Its negative qualities can be arrogance and pride.

On a physical level it is a tonic for depleted energy, helps to destroy bacteria, improves circulation, benefits hair, nails and skin and helps to alleviate rheumatism.

It is good for Living Rooms, Playrooms and any room where people come together. It would be good for using in large spaces, for conferences and seminars. It would also be good for Entrance Halls and Foyers. It is a colour that helps to calm aggression and give a sense of unity.

It goes very well with green, turquoise, aqua, blue, lilac and lavender.

Its complementary colour is Green.

We also need to consider the non-colours of black and white. When black pales to grey it may be useful as a calming neutral, but needs to be used with discretion as it has a hard quality and is associated with making one feel critical toward others, or oneself. It also has connotations of depression.

Pure black in decor is acceptable when used in small amounts, or used in furniture, but it can have very odd effects if used in any quantity as rooms painted black would seem to have no boundaries. So indefinable is black that it is often used to represent mystery, particularly in dress. When worn, or used by teenagers in their rooms, black shows that they have not yet defined their personality and do not want to be acknowledged, or defined, by the outward show of a particular colour. When we are older we may wear black when we are unsure of who we are or what we have become, although for men and women its weight-reducing effect is often taken into consideration.

White, on the other hand, symbolises bringing everything out into the light, and has connotations of purity, innocence, cleanliness and perfection. Often used as a symbol of luxury and elegance, since it takes wealth to keep a white environment looking pristine. It reflects the light and increases the apparent size of a room, but unless relieved by other colours, would look harsh and glaring in some lights and if overdone looks too clinical and sterile. Because we may have a hard time living up to the image of perfection inherent in white we may develop a sense of inferiority if we have to live with too much white on a daily basis.

There are, of course, many shades of white, and these can be used to good effect as they are not as stark as pure white.

What we need to strive for with colour in our homes is balance. Too much of any one colour can be overwhelming, and too little colour can be just plain boring. More importantly, however, is what suits us personally - what colours resonate with our personalities?

Colour is one area that has great relevance to the human subtle energy fields known esoterically as the Aura. When clairvoyants perceive the Aura they often see it in terms of swirling whorls of colour and each colour appears to denote a correlation to an emotion. This is perhaps why we unconsciously use to previously mentioned 'colour language', such as 'seeing red' or being 'in the pink', etc. These are the emotions that change rapidly depending on circumstances and mood, but underlying these are the habitual emotional patterns we live with from day to day. Clairvoyants would be able to 'read' from the colours dominant in our Aura the emotional world that we inhabit.

Red in the Aura shows different emotions depending upon the shade. In general, clear bright colours represent positive emotions and the muddy, greyer colours, the more negative emotions. Clear flame red shows a strong and socially orientated life force which emanates vitality and indicates a strong leader, who knows their own mind. Dull crimson may indicate someone who is intensely physical and who may often have eruptions of temper and a tendency toward violence. A lot of red flecks in the Aura indicates irritability.

Orange is another colour denoting general vitality and one who has fast reactions. People with a lot of orange are action dominated and may be interested in sports. It can denote flamboyancy, general sociability and goodwill and often shows a good imagination. Brown is not necessarily negative and can indicate someone who is very stable and earthy but who may have too much of a tendency for orderliness.

A clear yellow shows a strong intellect with a capacity for concentration. People with a lot of yellow are very capable and good at organising. Golden yellow shows an intellect moving toward the wisdom that is inspired and creative.

Muddy yellow shows a person who may desire to know things in order to use them to the disadvantage of someone else. It can be self-deceptive and cowardly.

Clear emerald green shows vitality of the heart, creativity and good-heartedness. Usually cheerful, optimistic and balanced, green people are often tuned into the natural world and may be drawn toward the healing arts.

Muddy greens indicate a treacherous nature, and one who may often lie and be generally deceitful.

Turquoise blue shows clarity of mind and a quick thinker. Again a healing colour and one that loves to communicate. Teachers may show this colour. It also shows the beginnings of a spiritual nature and turquoise people may be highly intuitive.

Blue shows honesty, integrity and reliability. Again a colour of clarity. Blue people are usually calm, trustworthy, farsighted and detached. They often have a refined nature, possibly veering toward the devotional life.

Muddy blues can indicate a tendency for depression.

Violet shows a creative and artistic nature which is often inspired and intuitive. A violet person may be contemplative and aspires to be spiritual. Violet people often have unusual minds and are willing to expand their thinking into unknown areas. Poetical and visionary, violet is almost 'other-worldly' but often denotes dignity.

The negative shades of violet may indicate someone who feels superior and proud and likes to exercise power over others.

Magenta shows a compassionate nature, one who is good at bringing people together and who empathises well with other people. Its negative connotation is arrogance.

Pure white is not common in the Aura and when it occurs shows a highly developed spiritual nature.

Black is usually an absence of a colour indicating possible damage or the start of a physical problem.

Grey is the colour that shows a tendency toward a critical nature and can also indicate fear and depression, which usually shows up as grey bands, like prison bars.

Whilst on the subject of the Aura we also need to briefly look at Chakras. Chakra is a Sanskrit word which means Wheel, and they look like vortexes of energy within the Aura that appear to absorb an 'electrical current' of life force energy into the body. They are sited at specific areas and connect with the glands of the endocrine system, the seven major plexuses where the main network of ganglia (nerve lines) are located, and with the vertebrae of the spine.

Each chakra absorbs a predominant colour and they are capable of opening and closing. See figure 7 for the correspondences of the seven main chakras. If you study the subject further you may find some differences in relation to the colours and correspondences as some esoteric schools of thought vary in their interpretation. In some cases the eight colours are related to eight chakras, with green connecting to the heart, turquoise corresponding with the Thymus Gland, blue for the throat, violet for the brow and magenta for the crown.

THE CHAKRAS

Chakra	Centre	Colour	Endocrine Gland	Qualities
1st	Base of Spine	Red	Adrenals	Security, Survival
2nd	Sacral (just below navel)	Orange	Gonads	Vitality, Pleasure, Sexuality
3rd	Solar Plexus	Yellow	Pancreas	Personal Emotions, Desire, Personal Power
4th	Heart	Green	Thymus	Love, Relationships, Compassion
5th	Throat	Blue	Thyroid	Communication, Self-expression
6th	Brow	Indigo	Pituitary	Intuition, Perception
7th	Crown	Violet	Pineal	Spiritual Awareness, Empathy

Figure 7

We also need to consider the effects of coloured lighting in the home. When using coloured lighting we are using a more powerful medium than with pigments. When we deal with pigments we are not dealing with 'real' colour but only with the representations of colour.

Coloured lighting can be used to subtly change or enhance the atmosphere of a room.

Red light is somewhat stimulating and increases self-awareness. This light will encourage witty remarks and teasing. It is sensual and sexual.

Orange light is stimulating and movement enhancing. It is very sociable and as previously mentioned is used in pubs for a more convivial atmosphere.

Yellow light has an uplifting effect, provided that the room contains plenty of everyday objects with a good balance of colour from the rest of the spectrum. It is not a good idea to use in a room already decorated in yellow.

Green light is not very pleasant as it can remind us of decay. It can, however, be used with good effect amongst green plants.

Turquoise light is cool and detached and will cool down the temperature.

Blue light has a much enhanced calming effect and can give a feeling of release and retreat into shelter.

Violet light creates peace and tranquillity and is particularly good for meditation.

Magenta light is very uplifting but it is very powerful and often gives a feeling of wanting to leave this world and its troubles so it needs careful handling, particularly if used in a magenta/violet environment.

Remember that Stage Designers have used coloured lighting to great effect to create mood and atmosphere but in the home this does need to be done with subtlety to avoid turning a room into the equivalent of a discotheque.

All the above information is offered as a guideline - it gives you the rules of harmony but these rules are not meant to be totally rigid. Be flexible and adventurous with easily changeable colours. Remember the neutral colours of grey, fawn, beige, cream and brown, and the non colours of white and black. Above all be guided by your own feelings of instinct and intuition, if you really love a colour then use it. Any you dislike then discard, but take a moment to look at the possible reasons for the dislike, it may be that it is a colour you have need of, if so you can always use it in another form, in food for example, to partake of its energy.

Take into account those who share your home and their likes and dislikes. Remember too that good design with colour is strongly connected to form, line, shape and texture. But above all remember to enjoy colour as a medium of expression, creativity and artistry.

There has literally been an explosion in the use of colour since the 1960's. It is not, however, always used wisely. Many companies use Colour Consultants to help them create and project an image and to help sell their products. Because colour is so intimately linked to the emotions you obviously need to be aware of this to avoid being manipulated.

Understand colour and then you have dominion over it and you have another area in your life that empowers you and helps make you whole, for colour is nourishment for our subtle energies as well as a reflection of what we truly are.

CHAPTER 6

SOUND AND MUSIC

Sound, as with Light and Colour, works on many levels of our awareness, both consciously and unconsciously. In our homes we have a certain amount of control over the sounds we generate but have very little control over external sounds. If we are able to we can avoid buying or renting a house near obvious sources of problematic sound such as an airport, railway line, motorway, busy road, etc., although no-one knows what may be built in your locality in the future. If we live in such an area already all we can do is to figure out methods of keeping the sound out. However we can get ourselves into a Catch 22 situation where by insulating against sound we rob ourselves of necessary ventilation.

Unwanted sound or noise, which is sound 'gone wild' and out of harmony has become an increasing problem as we 'progress' in our 20th Century. The noise of aircraft, traffic, construction, road repairs, are all relatively recent phenomena and we are not coping very well with this additional burden of noise.

Indoors, with the advent of electrical gadgets, particularly the almost constant hum of refrigerators and freezers, finds us unable to experience the healing sounds of silence. Silence that is not absolute, (which can be just as disturbing) but a living silence that allows for listening to the sigh of the wind and the singing of the birds.

So what is the nature of sound. We are immersed in an ocean of sound and only hear a small proportion of this sound with our ears. Sound is vibrational motion - the motion of atoms and molecules oscillating.

Theo Gimbel, Colour Therapist and researcher, in his book Healing with Colour, has suggested that there are five steps into manifested form - Darkness, Light, Colour, Sound and Form, and that sound is the powerful means by which form is created, first at an energy level and then into physical manifestation. This is perhaps the idea behind the words in the Bible - In the Beginning was the Word. It was suggested by Goethe that architecture was frozen music and others have suggested that crystals are frozen sound.

Ernst Chladni, an 18th Century German Physicist, demonstrated that sound waves could create patterns by using a violin bow to vibrate on metal plates that were covered with grains of sand. He discovered that distinct patterns were determined by the pitch of the note, as well as the size and thickness of the oscillating plates.

In the 1960's the German Physicist and musician, Hans Jenny, also studied the effects of sounds on many different substances such as powders, liquids and semi-solids such as mercury and glycerine gel. Using similar methods to Chladni, he discovered that the wave energy of sounds created patterns that were geometrical and abstract but that also showed the patterns generally found in nature, such as leaf structures and spirals. He discovered how the pitch controlled the patterns, the low pitches making wider and larger patterns and the higher pitches forming very fine and intricate patterns.

To produce sound an object has to vibrate, or move to and fro. A guitar string, for example, vibrates to and fro hundreds of times a second and each complete to and fro is 1 cycle. The number of cycles the string vibrates in a second is the frequency, measured in units called Hertz, abbreviated to Hz, 1 Hz, then is 1 cycle per second.

When these frequencies rise above 20 Hz the human ear detects them and translates the noise as one continuous sound. Lower than this the ear detects individual cycles and below 17 Hz this becomes a vibration that is felt rather than heard and is known as Infrasound. Low pitched sounds, like the sound of thunder, have low frequencies and high pitched sounds have high frequencies.

It has been suggested that very low frequency sounds, below 20 Hz may have the ability to destroy structure and form and even cells, and that very high frequency noise may cause insanity in humans. The frequency of human conversation is generally in the range of 200-400 Hz, so the note called Middle C (the Pythagorean Middle C) of 256 Hz is roughly in the centre of this frequency.

Animals such as cats, bats, dogs and dolphins have a wide range of hearing, extending to 200,000 Hz and above. Humans are generally unable to detect sounds with frequencies above about 20,000 Hz. Sounds that have frequencies too high for us to hear are known as Ultrasonic. Even though we only hear this range of frequencies with our ears it is possible that the whole frequency range of sound in the spectrum has an effect on our bodies at a cellular or molecular level.

The loudness of a sound depends upon the amount of movement in the vibrations. Slight movement represents a soft sound and vigorous movement, a loud sound. This volume of sound is measured in units called decibels (dB). Conversation is usually around 60 dB, at below 20 dB humans cannot detect sound, and the pain threshold of sound starts at around 120 dB. During the 1960's it was a common rumour that if you took an egg with you to a Rock Concert and were able to place it on or near the stage, by the end of the concert the egg would have become hard-boiled, just by the effects of the sound.

We also need to take into account the phenomenon known as resonance. If two or more objects are tuned to the same natural frequency of vibration and one of them produces a sound, the other will also vibrate as a result of the sound waves emitted by the first object. This is a sympathetic vibration and is called acoustic resonance. Physics defines resonance as the interaction of two 'bodies' vibrating at about the same frequency.

So now that we have a greater understanding of sound, what action can we take about unwanted noise. In some instances it may be possible to improve a given situation. For example, if there is land available between a noise source and your house you may be able to create an earth berm (a mound of soil planted with shrubs), or plant rows of thick trees or shrubs that will help minimise the effects of the noise by reflecting and absorbing it. A fence may do the same thing. The best shrubs are those with thick fleshy leaves and thin leaf stalks that allow flexibility, and with trees, obviously the taller the trees and wider the area covered, the better the effect. Evergreens, of course, are effective all year round.

Airborne sound is carried in the air and enters the house through open windows and doors and through small cracks and gaps. You can block up the cracks and gaps, but as previously mentioned, this may be at the cost of natural ventilation. Double glazing can be helpful to keep out sound but ideally needs a wider gap between the panes than for energy conservation. Remember also that if you exclude too much sound the result may be oppressively quiet and tend to produce feelings of isolation and unease.

Impact sounds occur when you drop an object onto the floor which causes vibration to travel through floors and walls to be heard loudly on the other side. Refrigerators, freezers, washing machines, etc, fall into this category as well as the direct sounds category, because the vibrations from these machines often transmit through floors and walls. Even distant impact sounds can be heard. Remember the noise railway lines make even when the train is a long way off. This is known as flanking sound.

Problems often arise in flats where there is not enough mass in the partitioning walls, thereby allowing noise from neighbouring flats to become intrusive. Likewise through floors. This can only be solved by adding a second, independent, inner-frame wall covered with a double layer of plasterboard. It is also possible to construct a 'floating floor' by laying a dense mineral fibre quilt and fixing floorboards to battens on top. A ceiling could also be lined by using a quilt of fibre, battens and plasterboard. You may need some expert help and advice with these sort of modifications.

Noisy indoor machines like refrigerators could be placed on thick rubber mats or by moving such appliances into a utility area outside of the kitchen.

Living and sleeping areas really need to be placed in the quietest parts of the house if this is at all possible.

Remember that direct sounds reflect off surfaces so predominantly hard surfaces and bare floors will tend to echo. This is fine if you like the spacious effect it can give, but if you wish to feel cosier and more intimate you could use thick curtains and carpets or rugs, fabric wall hangings or even line walls with a fabric such as hessian. This creates absorbent surfaces.

Sounds can be loud, piercing or sharp. They can soothe, invigorate or depress and they can generally stir the emotions by disorientating, or uplifting us. In some way they have an effect on our well-being. One of the ways we can mitigate these effects is to use another sound to help mask the unwanted ones. We also need to understand that the impact of sound is not entirely a function of how loud it is. Psychologically any noise is tolerated more easily if we have direct control over it, or if it has some relation to the listener, and even when it is perceived as having a positive effect. Our lawnmower does not bother us as much as our neighbours, nor does our barking dog or crying baby. When we use the food-processor, for instance, we know it is only noisy whilst it is achieving something on our behalf, and it is under our direct control so it is not quite such a problem.

What we are aiming for in a healing home is a peaceful environment rather than sustained extreme silence. We need sounds that will energise us when we require energising and relax us when we require relaxation. We can also bring the sounds of nature into or near our homes and these have the additional benefit of linking us to the natural world and helping us to renew our connection to the earth. We could, for example, put a bird feeder or bird bath near a window or plant trees and shrubs that attract the birds. Birdsong is usually a delightful sound.

Plants such as bamboo only require a slight breeze to give a rustling sound and these breezes can also create sounds if you hang something that moves in the wind. Windchimes and bells, wind flutes or even paper streamers all have their own distinctive and pleasing sounds. The most ethereal of these is made by the Aeolian Harp. This device consists of a series of tuneable strings stretched across a sound box and as the wind eddy passes over the strings they vibrate and generate a subtle, and sometimes eerie, sound. Windchimes can also be hung near doors or open windows indoors, although I have to confess to a personal passion for windchimes and have them wherever I pass frequently by so I can touch them and hear the different sounds.

The sound of moving water too is very atmospheric and uplifting. We can place a pond in our gardens which will attract croaking frogs and a waterfall or fountain makes a lovely evocative sound. If you do not have the space for an outdoor pool or fountain, there are small fountains and waterfalls that have a recirculating pump which are ideal for indoor use. One of my favourite possessions is a Ceramic waterfall which has afforded me many hours of relaxed pleasure, as well as providing an unusual focal point for the room.

It is also possible nowadays to buy recordings of nature sounds. The sound of ocean waves, rainstorms, whales and dolphins, birds, etc, are all available to us on tape. And then, of course, we have a vast array of music available to us which we can utilise to aid relaxation and meditation, concentration, creativity, healing and positive mental states.

Whereas noise is sound 'gone wild' and randomised, music is harmonised, structured sound. It generally pleases our ears. Music is a universal human language and people have used musical sounds for pleasure, for magic, and for healing, throughout the centuries. It is said that Lord Krishna, a member of the Hindu Deic Trinity, used the music of the flute to promote the green verdant beauty in the Indian city of Vrindaven. One of the ten sages of the Court of the famous Moghul Emperor, Akbar, who was called Mion Tan Sen, was reputed to be able to perform miracles with his songs and could bring on rain or induce plants to blossom by intoning devotional songs or ragas at them.

In their book, *The Secret Life of Plants*, Peter Tompkins and Christopher Bird described the experiments carried out by Dorothy Rettalack of Denver in 1968. These experiments were part of her studies in biology and she chose to study the effect of music on plants which produced some interesting results.

Beethoven and other 18th Century composers had a positive effect (ie the plants grew better than the control group) but the 'acid rock' music of the day had a detrimental effect on the plants. The jazz music of Ellington and Armstrong had a positive effect whilst folk and country and western music had a completely neutral effect. However, the music that had the greatest positive response was the classical Indian music of Ravi Shankar playing the sitar.

Research has been conducted over the years on the effect of playing music to crops and it appears possible that plant growth is strongly affected by particular types of music. It has even been suggested that birdsong, so prevalent in the Spring, has a direct and beneficial effect on the new growth of plants.

In ancient Egypt, the hieroglyph for music was the same as that for joy and well-being. The work of Pythagoras, in Classical Greece, regarded physical form as the manifestation of music, and he had a profound understanding of the proportions and harmonics of music. In 324 BC the music of the Lyre was supposed to have restored Alexander the Great to sanity, and in the Old Testament, David played his harp to lift the depression afflicting King Saul.

In ancient Tibet, the religion that preceded Buddhism called Bön (Buddhism reaching Tibet in the 7th or 8th Century) understood and utilised the healing and therapeutic effects of sound and music, as well as light and colour.

The Singing Bowls of Tibet were supposed to have been developed during this time and these were made from an alloy of seven sacred metals thought to be Gold, Silver, Copper, Zinc, Tin, Lead and Iron. These bowls can either be struck to give a wonderful bell-like sound, or they are 'sung' by rubbing the outside of the bowl with a wooden stick. This produces an incredible sound that is supposed to be deeply healing.

It has been shown through scientific studies that resonance is a crucial factor when healing with sound and music. As the sound waves enter the body, sympathetic vibrations are set up in the living cells, which appear to restore them to healthy reorganisation. As the high water content of the body's tissues helps to conduct sound, it is possible that the effect of sound upon the body is like a massage on the cellular level. This is possibly how the Tibetan Singing Bowls work as they were made in many different sizes that have different resonances.

In modern times Quartz Singing Bowls have been created. These bowls are made from Silicon Sand, so pure it is used to make fibre optic glass. This sand is dropped into a spinning mould containing an electric arc torch burning at several thousand degrees centigrade which integrates the individual particles into a unified whole. The bowls are then tuned. These bowls are played in the same way as the Tibetan bowls using a rubber headed stick.

Interestingly quartz crystal was used in a healing musical instrument made by Benjamin Franklin in the 1700's. The idea was derived from the tapping of glasses to produce musical sounds and later models were known as the Glass Harmonica or Armonicum which became very popular in the early 1800's. Unfortunately, the material used in these later models was not quartz but glass made with a lead content which was found to be detrimental to health, so the instrument lost popularity.

In 1982, Gerhard Finkenbeiner in Massachusetts, was inspired to rebuild this instrument using natural quartz crystal. This instrument had an overall beneficial effect with no problematic side effects. Finkenbeiner also started building quartz crystal church bells. It is said that in the legendary days of Lemuria, which preceded Atlantis, quartz crystal flutes, which had a high degree of resonancy, were used for healing.

Chants and mantras have also been used throughout recorded history for their beneficial and therapeutic qualities. Accumulated energy is supposed to reside in the mantric sound which through age and repetition gathers a 'life of its own'. The most well known mantra is the sacred word Om (Aum) sometimes called 'the first mantra'. Mantras are also used in meditation.

Chanting is now growing in popularity and can provide the experience of vitalising the body's energy. There are also special chanting techniques such as Overtone Chanting which is highly valued as a therapeutic tool. Overtone Chanting is centuries old but it is a technique not easily acquired. Overtones exist in every vocal sound and are sets of harmonic frequencies related to the main pitch, or note, of the sound.

The music that came out of the heart of Africa symbolises rhythmic vitality. Drums were, and still are, made from all manner of materials and form a vital part of tribal life. Indeed in countries such as Ghana, rhythm and culture are so intimately linked that you cannot even discuss one without the other. In Ghana, with its monarchical traditions, royal drums are very important. The royal drums of Ghana are the Obonu Drums and the Royal Households are also the homes of each nation's Obuno Drums. Each nation has its own rhythms which are uniquely theirs, and it is only in recent years that the Twelve Royal Houses of Ghana have consented to allow their drums and drum rhythms to be performed together abroad.

Music is also central to the lives of the Baka pygmies who live in the forests of the Southeast Cameroon. It unites the group, and is used for charming animals to ensure the success of the hunt, for telling stories, for healing illness or misfortune and above all for fun. Martin Cradick and his wife, Su Hart, were inspired by a Channel 4 documentary about the Baka and their music and eventually were able to spend time with them in the forest. From this came an album called Spirit of the Forest by Baka Beyond which fuses the Baka music with Martin's own compositions. I was fortunate enough to see and hear them play live at the 1994 WOMAD Festival, a festival that brings together, and celebrates, World Music.

Rhythm, according to the New Age Composer and Musician, Lasos, provides nourishment and he says that "rhythm is an 'energy pump' through time", which is capable of pumping energy into the body, vitalising it.

In many cultures each craft of the countryside had their own rhythms and songs which reflected the body movements made by that craft. It is well known that the rowers of ancient sailing craft were encouraged to row in unison and given strength by the rhythm of a drum beat or with a particular song. You only have to think of the Volga Boatmen song to get the idea.

Out of the intervals and rhythmic elements, as well as the changes of pitch, the melody or tune is finally created. These melodies can have the effect of making us happy, sometimes they can be slow and soothing, or at times, disturbing and discordant.

Cyril Scott, author of *Music, Its Secret Influence Throughout the Ages*, suggested that the whole purpose of dissonant or discordant music, found in the many forms of modern music, was to break up thought forms which had crystallised into too rigid a pattern, which may explain why the music of the 1960's had such a profound effect on society.

The present day concert pitch is 264 Hz, almost half a tone (about 8 Hz) above the old Pythagorean pitch, which made Middle C 256 Hz. Theo Gimbel's research has shown that young children taught music are frequently said to be unmusical because they cannot find their notes easily. Using the old Pythagorean pitch they can find their notes. He maintains that the whole body of each human being is aligned to the pitch of 256 Hz for Middle C and as children are still unspoilt they find this pitch more natural. This may also explain why I had difficulty singing at school as the pitch always seemed too high for my voice.

When Pythagoras talked about music he was referring not to the melody, but to a pattern or rhythm of energy. In his early works he states that - all things are constructed on harmonious patterns - therefore when we are out of step with natural harmony, disharmony arises. The principles of bringing into harmony different oscillating frequencies underlies all methods of vibrational healing, such as the use of colour, sound, music, crystals, homeopathic remedies, etc.

Music is also used by therapists and healers because music enhances our ability to evoke visual imagery which also plays a part in harmonising our energies.

The Chakra system mentioned in the previous chapter also corresponds to musical notes, although once again you may find discrepancies between the different systems.

1st Chakra	-	the Key of C
2nd Chakra	-	the Key of D
3rd Chakra	-	the Key of E
4th Chakra	-	the Key of F
5th Chakra	-	the Key of G
6th Chakra	-	the Key of A
7th Chakra	-	the Key of B

The choice of music you play is very individual and it is very difficult to generalise about what makes good healing music. The current trend for New Age and 'healing' music is very welcome and there are many fine pieces of music available. It may be however, that someone suffering from depression would require a more up-tempo piece of music to energise them and to lift their spirits. I personally find more richness and variety in World Music and can usually find pieces in this field to suit or create a particular mood. There are also some pieces of classical music that are wonderfully healing. The music of Debussy I find connects me to the world of nature more than any other music I have heard.

Interestingly, Cyril Scott in *Music, Its Secret Influence Throughout the Ages*, tells us that Debussy was inspired by the intelligences inherent within nature to write his music and that it equates to the beautiful colour of Apple Green. Cesar Frank and Alexander Scriabin were also supposed to be inspired by the higher realms and the music of Bach is said to have led to a leap in the mental faculties of humanity.

So it would appear that music and rhythm reflect the pulse of life and it could be said that to the extent that we ourselves respond to the rhythms of music, we are also responding to the rhythms of the natural universe which resonates through our being, bringing harmony to the deepest level of ourselves.

Whatever the inspiration behind the various types of music, this is an area where we have freedom of choice and can enrich and enhance the quality of our lives by the wise use of music.

Also we must not forget how much fun and joy we can gain through playing a musical instrument or by singing. After all the voice is an incredible instrument and singing tones up the body wonderfully well. Even if you have no musical training it is possible to enjoy yourself by drumming on home-made drums which can help you establish and strengthen the rhythmic patterns of your body. Such instruments also allow for an emotional release and encourages movement and agility.

Whatever the motives for playing or listening to music the prime reason is really to bring us joy - for music is life.

CHAPTER 7

FENG SHUI AND THE ART OF PLACEMENT

Feng Shui, (pronounced Fung Shway) literally translated as Wind-Water, is the ancient Chinese geomantic art of placement. It has been referred to as Mystical Interior Design and its general aim is to enable us to be in tune with our surroundings. This is achieved by bringing together the external and internal environment into a balanced whole.

Feng Shui is rapidly becoming popular in the West, partly in response to the growing interest in the use of Chinese Medicine. Just as Chinese Medicine involves the interplay of balance between Yin (passive) and Yang (active), which are the two extremes of the same energy, and acupuncture is based upon the notion of energy meridians which permeate the physical body and carry the vital force called Ch'i, the Chinese also understood that the earth has her own energy channels that circulate the Ch'i force. The Ch'i force is described as the Cosmic Breath or energy ascribed to the atmosphere, the earth and humans. This is the most important aspect that Feng Shui practitioners seek to alter as they channel Ch'i to enhance and improve human Ch'i and thus increase happiness, prosperity and vitality.

Chinese Medicine and Feng Shui also work with the theory of Yin and Yang, the Taoist concept that unites all opposites. The symbol of the Yin/Yang energies (see Chapter illustration) clearly shows the polarity of light and dark; black and white; in a dancing, oscillating circle, each containing the seed potential of the other - portrayed by the small black circle in the white area, and vice versa. This symbolises the balance between the two extremes that we are always striving for. Only a balanced interplay of energies will lead us to harmony. This does not imply a stagnant separation of two equal parts, but a moving, dynamic whole - the blending and mixing of two polarities to create a third energy which is the synergy we call harmony.

In our personal lives one of the greatest challenges we face is the balancing of the polarities of the female and male energies. The feminine energy tends toward Yin and the masculine tends toward Yang. When we are born we come into focus in one polarity or another, whereby we are predominantly more one energy than the other, and the cultural conditioning of our time prefers that we stay in either one or the other.

This leads to great confusion because we have forgotten that each human being does, in fact, contain both these energies but chooses one as a focus with the aim of working through this one focus, whilst utilising the other polarity, to give a balanced human being. At the moment it is easier to be a 'real' man, or woman, but only half a human being.

The feminine energy is creative and has the ability to 'set the scene' and create ambience. The masculine energy is one of action and doing which takes place within the setting created by the feminine energy. One is not better than the other because they are both a polarity of the same energy and cannot exist alone.

Because culturally women have only been allowed to express the feminine energy, it is usually women who create the home environment - they set the scene and often have an innate sense of placement and the rightness of a setting. This may explain why some women are often to be found, once more, rearranging the furniture. They are at a deeper level sensing that a change of energy is required, and by moving the furniture around a change of energy will occur. They instinctively know what feels right so that the Ch'i will flow in a different way.

Of course, there are men who access their feminine polarity and are excellent at interior design and the art of placement, as there are women who are successful at calling upon their masculine energy to take action. This does not mean that they necessarily have to be gay, nor that every gay man or woman is successfully accessing their polarity. There does seem to be a blurring of sexual identities at this time, which may, possibly, be a response to the overwhelming imbalance between the feminine and masculine energies, although I am sure there are many other factors to be taken into consideration.

Whilst the Chinese art of placement, Feng Shui, is definitely worth looking into and utilising, we do need to remember, however, that it has been developed over centuries in its own cultural setting and what may be symbolic and meaningful to an oriental person may not quite translate into a western mentality. Despite this there is usually a definite effect if you follow some of the guidelines of Feng Shui.

A household word in many parts of Asia, Feng Shui is a cross between an art and a science and its goal is to arrange buildings, rooms and furniture in the most beneficial way and thus achieve greater harmony with nature. When this is done, prosperity and happiness are sure to follow. People in Asia generally have an understanding of the basic rules of Feng Shui but would usually call upon the services of a Feng Shui Master who has studied the subject in great depth. Feng Shui is a product of early Chinese thought and is a mix of the yin/yang theory of balance and oneness with nature, common sense and superstition. It is still used extensively by ordinary Asian people but has become increasingly popular with the business community in Hong Kong, Singapore and Taiwan and is spreading across the Western world.

Traditional Feng Shui Masters used a special compass called a lo p'an, and other divining tools, and were originally called upon to locate the most auspicious site for the tomb of a departed loved one. This lo p'an had a compass built into its centre, working on the theory that the magnetic effects and the flow of Ch'i in the environment could be measured and described accurately. This compass is extremely complicated and is based upon the divisions of the solar year, the zodiac circle, the eight trigrams of the I Ching (Book of Change) the five elements and many others. Over time the practice of classical Feng Shui grew to include a detailed observation of the living world and the way in which the earth energy affected all of our daily life.

The Feng Shui practitioner also considers four dimensions:

Ch'i - the vital or life force energy, composed of both Yin/Yang elements, the generative force in the universe

Li - the natural laws of the universe such as astrology, orientation according to the four directions and honouring the ancestors

So - the mathematical relationships which explain the
        workings behind nature

Ying - the natural history of a place, particularly its
        landforms and the behaviour of animals.

In the more modern intuitive Feng Shui, sometimes called Black
Hat Feng Shui, the practitioner applies the principles of the I
Ching Ba-gua. The Ba-gua is an Octagon grid (see figure 8)
which divides into eight life situations; marriage, fame, wealth,
family, knowledge, career, helpful people and children. This Ba-
gua is simply superimposed on a building or individual room
and all that is needed to properly align the Ba-gua is to
determine the location of the front door. The door, called the
Ch'i Kou, is literally translated as the mouth of Ch'i and no
matter how seldom the front door is used it is still considered
the main door to calculate the Ba-gua position. The Black Hat
sect of Feng Shui differs from the traditional practice where a
fixed Ba-gua is superimposed on the property, where the area of
Li (fame) would always be south.

When we orientate the Ba-gua with the location of the front
door, the door will fall into one of three categories, either Gen
(knowledge), Ken (career) or Chyan (helpful people). Because
rooms and apartments often present a variety of shapes the Ba-
gua can be elongated or shortened in order to apply to each
shape (see figure 9).

To give an idea of how you can utilise the Ba-gua, consider a
house that is L-shaped, in other words a section of the Ba-gua
appears to be missing. This section may fall in the marriage
area or the wealth area for example, and may indicate that
those areas in your life are causing you problems.

Feng Shui offers two ways to solve our problems. One is called
Ru-shr and is logical, reasonable and rational and is within our
range of knowledge and experience. The other is Chu-shr - the
use of the illogical, irrational, transcendental and mystical - that
which may be beyond our comprehension. These two blend

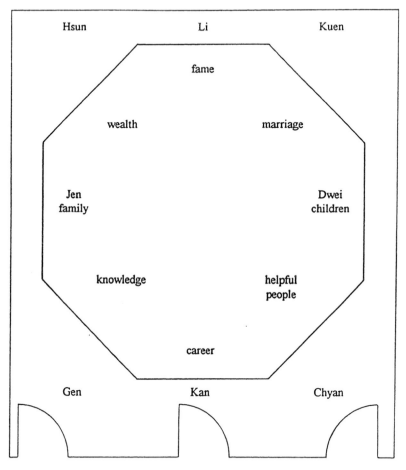

Hsun   Li   Kuen

fame

wealth   marriage

Jen
family   Dwei
children

knowledge   helpful
people

career

Gen   Kan   Chyan

The three possible entrances

Fig 8 Ba-Gua

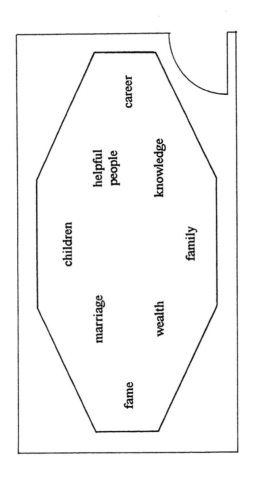

Fig 9 Elongated Ba-Gua

together in the nine basic cures, or remedies, to alter, moderate or raise Ch'i. The nine cures are:

1.   Bright or light reflecting objects such as mirrors, crystal balls or lights.

2.   Sounds - windchimes, bells, etc.

3.   Living Objects - plants, flowers, fish in aquariums, etc.

4.   Moving objects - mobiles, windmills and fountains.

5.   Heavy objects - stones or statues.

6.   Electronically powered objects, stereo, TV, etc.

7.   Bamboo Flutes.

8.   Colours.

9.   Others - ranging from ribbons, tassels, fringes and symbols.

Back to our L-shaped house with the missing section. We can apply one or more of the cures to this situation. We could, for example, place a large stone or statue externally, at the corner where the walls would have met if it was a square or a rectangular shape. We could also mark off the area in some way and then define the area outside to give the impression of being part of the house. It could be planted with trees, shrubs and flowers, so that it is generally viewed in a favourable way. Or we could install a light at the 'missing' corner.

Doors that open inward are beneficial as they allow the Ch'i to enter and windchimes in the doorway are also considered auspicious.

Corridors that run from the front to the back of the house require correcting as the Ch'i may not circulate around the house. In some cases a Ying Pei (spirit screen) is suggested, literally a little wall built behind the front door.

Rooms that run the whole length of the house from front to back need correcting by using furniture or screens to divide the room and slow down the Ch'i.

Staircases that run up directly behind the door are not ideal. They are better toward the rear of the building on a side wall with a landing or change or direction half way up. The suggested correction is to hang a curtain across the bottom of the stairs.

Sharp corners that jut out at you, particularly in relation to the bed, are not considered good, but can be easily corrected by hanging a plant, windchime or mobile in front of the corner.

Beams are considered somewhat oppressive but this can be offset by hanging something from them.

Mirrors are almost considered to be the aspirin of Feng Shui and can be used in many ways and positions to enhance and enliven Ch'i. If you have a wall with pipes running down, which are boxed in, possibly blocking off a corner, you can solve the problem by placing a mirror on the blocked off wall.

Outside you may need to deflect threatening Ch'i, for example, from a road that aims straight at the house, or an overpoweringly tall building near by. Mirrors could be used to deflect the Ch'i.

Mirrors should be large enough and correctly positioned so as not to 'cut off' the top of a person's head. They should also be hung in one piece and not used as little mirrored pieces which distort images. Mirrors can also reflect intruders to anyone whose back is to the door.

Aquariums with bubbling aerators and fountains stimulate Ch'i and fish further enrich a home and are used to absorb accidents and general bad luck. When they die they should immediately be replaced (not so lucky for the fish though!).

I am not going into too much detail on this rather complex subject as there are books on Feng Shui, or you can call upon the services of a Feng Shui practitioner.

It is also possible for you to just take a good look at your home and intuit, or feel, the energies around you and then develop your own version of Feng Shui.

If I buy something new for the home I do not always know exactly where to put it. What I do is try it out somewhere and if the first position does not feel right in relation to me or the energy in the room, I keep moving it about, often moving many other elements at the same time, until I find the mix that gives the right energy. This does not have to be strictly symmetrical or conform to any particular rule of design, it just has to be comfortable, pleasing to the eye, and quite simply feel right.

Experiment and see for yourself, you may be surprised how good you are at the art of placement.

CHAPTER 8

AIR, EARTH, FIRE AND WATER

Everything that exists on the planet is composed of the four elements of air, earth, fire and water and our homes are no exception.

The very existence of the element of air is something we take for granted. It is composed of roughly 78% nitrogen and 21% oxygen with a small amount of other gases. This is a fairly precise proportion, vary the nitrogen or oxygen by only a few percent and all life on earth would be put at risk. Part of James

Lovelock's Gaia hypothesis maintains that this balance is designed specifically for living things and it is the perfect medium for creating and sustaining life.

The process of breathing is automatic and on average we take between 20 and 40 breaths per minute. The lungs are a sophisticated processing plant filtering the air you inhale, absorbing oxygen into the bloodstream and expelling carbon dioxide.

Many ancient religions and teachings see the breath and correct breathing as central to physical and spiritual well-being. The air itself contains the vital life force, known as Prana in ancient Indian teachings, which is another way of referring to the Ch'i force of the Chinese. This Prana is part of the living air and is dependant upon air quality and sunlight. Sunlight literally 'charges up' the air with dancing, vibrating particles, known in esoteric terms as 'Vitality Globules'. These globules are said to be due to an infusion of the chemical oxygen with Prana, from within, and they are visible to the naked eye. Choose a sunny day when there is blue sky above and without looking in the direction of the sun, look up into the hazy blue. Let your eyes go slightly out of focus and with a bit of practise and time you realise you are looking at hundreds of minute specks of light, dancing and moving with extreme rapidity. They seem to come into being and disappear after a few seconds. These specks are not to be confused with the tiny slow moving circles floating on the surface of your eye. You can tell that these particles are external to you and they permeate the whole atmosphere. You cannot see them indoors, and on a cloudy day, whilst they are still visible, they are not so abundant, nor do they move as rapidly. If these particles are connected to the life force energy, which appears to be related to sunlight, this may explain why we tend to feel lethargic after a few days of cloudy weather.

In earlier centuries we did not have to be too concerned about the quality of our air. We spent more time outdoors and were not worried by the smoke of the Industrial Revolution, or by the chemical pollution of modern times. 'Clean Air' legislation in some of the industrialised countries has reduced smoke pollution, but city air is now becoming increasingly contaminated by sulphur dioxide from power plants and carbon monoxide and nitrogen oxides which are a legacy of our increasing use of motor vehicles.

A lot of our time these days is spent indoors and it is a startling fact that most indoor pollution does not come from outside but is generated within. This is a result of the widespread use of synthetic building materials, finishes, fabrics, furnishings, and household chemicals. Taken together with the pollutants such as dust, bacteria and fungi, we have created a situation whereby more and more people are suffering from asthma, hay fever and related respiratory allergies or illnesses.

This situation has not been improved with the current trend for energy conservation where we seal all the gaps in the structure of our homes, around the doors and windows, etc, thus reducing the amount of ventilation.

Another health risk that we are recently becoming aware of is the existence of radon. Radon is a natural substance that is a tasteless, odourless, invisible gas which varies enormously in concentration in different regions of the world. This gas is giving problems now due to our desire to keep heat, and thereby air, and Radon, in. You can contact your local health department to establish whether you live in a Radon area, the levels of Radon in your home and what appropriate local remedial actions are available.

When houses are built with natural materials such as brick (without cavity wall insulation), stone, timber and plaster, there is a natural diffusion of air through these porous materials. This ventilation by diffusion is advantageous because the porous materials help absorb and release excess moisture, helping to regulate indoor humidity and to expel pollutants.

One of the ways to deal with poor air quality is to find the main sources of pollution, remove or restrict them, and increase the level of natural ventilation. The expensive way is to invest in complex mechanical ventilation and filtration systems. Portable filters are also available but may not be quite so effective.

Another factor of air quality is ionisation. In unpolluted outdoor places, especially in the mountains or by waterfalls, the air contains from 1000 to 2000 ions per cubic centimetre, in a ratio of five positive to four negative. This balance gives us a general feeling of well-being. Where there is a surfeit of positive ions, for example, just before a thunderstorm, or during winds such as the 'Mistral' in France, or the 'Sharav' of the Middle East, unpleasant feelings of tension, irritability and depression can develop.

Inside the home, negative ions are depleted by electrical fields from televisions, VDU's and static from synthetic fabrics. It is now possible to buy negative ion generators, usually just called ionisers which also help to remove smoke, dust and some allergens. Many users of these ionisers are convinced that they are very helpful although there is no consensus among researchers that ion concentrations in the air significantly affects well-being.

Another area where we can positively enhance air quality is through the use of natural fragrances. Our sense of smell is many thousand times more acute than our sense of taste and acts directly on certain areas of the brain. Because of this, fragrance is extremely evocative and is linked to our emotions, thereby influencing our mood.

Psychologists are now attaching greater importance to fragrance and its beneficial effects. Many fragrances have an effect due to association and memory. A favourite Aunt who always wore Lavender, the smell of freshly baked bread, the heady scent of flowers in summer, may well trigger old and pleasant memories, whilst unpleasant memories, such as a stay in hospital, are just as easily triggered by such smells as ether and disinfectant. This could be because the area of the brain known as the limbic system contains the main centres for both memory and olfaction.

This area is sometimes referred to as the 'old brain' and was one of the first parts to develop in our early ancestors.

The connection between odours, the brain, and feelings was recognised by ancient cultures. In ancient Greece, aromatic oils were often employed for their soporific, antidepressant or aphrodisiac properties, and it was understood that certain odours could improve mental alertness and concentration.

Research over the years has suggested that we need odour stimulation for aesthetic and spiritual well-being, almost as if the brain needs information in this form. This could be because the sense of smell is the only sense in which the receptor nerve endings are in direct contact with the outside world, in other words, your brain extends directly into your nose. Also, olfactory nerve cells are the only type of nerve cell in the body which can be replaced if damaged so they must surely be important.

We know, of course, that the human nose quickly gets use to an odour and will appear not to notice it after a while, but it seems that odours still affect us even when we do not consciously perceive them.

As well as directly affecting our feelings via the brain, fragrances may well act directly on the subtle energy field in ways we do not yet understand.

One of the best ways to fragrance the house is to use essential oils. Essential oils are used in the healing art of Aromatherapy which we will be discussing in a later chapter.

Essential oils are extremely concentrated liquids that are extracted from flowers, leaves, roots, seeds, barks and resins. They need to be bought from a reputable supplier as it is very easy for them to be adulterated, and because most essential oils are expensive there are quite a lot of adulterated oils on the market. However, since they are so concentrated it is possible to buy small amounts relatively inexpensively and a few drops is all that is required. A further bonus of these oils is the fact that many of them are good antibacterial agents.

To create an uplifting mood, or to help dispel depression use a citrus oil such as Orange or Lemon, or Jasmine, Lavender, Bergamot, Rose, Sandalwood or Ylang Ylang.

To help alleviate anxiety and calm stress, use Bergamot, Lavender or Geranium. To create a peaceful environment and to offset anger, impatience and irritability, try Chamomile, Melissa (Lemon Balm), Rose, Ylang Ylang or Frankincense.

To help give clarity of mind use citrus oils or Peppermint. Rose, Jasmine, Neroli and Ylang Ylang are sensuous fragrances ideal for the bedroom. Frankincense and Sandalwood are useful for creating a contemplative or meditative mood.

To fragrance a room you can use an oil burner, usually a ceramic bowl which has space underneath for a 'night light' candle. You put water into the bowl, light the candle and add one or two drops of the chosen essential oil. You do need to keep a careful watch on the candle but it does not take long for the fragrance to diffuse throughout the room.

You may also wish to add a few drops to water in a spray bottle or atomiser. This can either be used for spraying into the air or for wiping over surfaces to keep them clean and smelling good.

Another way to bring fragrance into your home is by the use of incense. This is becoming increasingly popular nowadays, although it has been used for many thousands of years for magical, spiritual and religious purposes. It started to become popular in the West in the 1960's and was part of the 'hippy culture' of that time, mostly being referred to as joss sticks.

It was burned in antiquity, possibly to mask the odours of the sacrifice of animals, and to carry prayers to the gods. It was, and still is, used to promote a particular state of consciousness or to enhance the atmosphere and change mood. The smoke from incense, in common with all things, possesses specific vibrational rates which act upon our subtle energy fields as well as our emotions. Even the word perfume is derived from Latin, meaning 'through the smoke'.

Incense is composed of a variety of leaves, flowers, roots, woods, resins, gums and oils and is generally made into either incense sticks or cones which are combustible, or is loosely packed into jars and requires the use of a burning charcoal block onto which it is sprinkled.

We shall look at another method of fragrancing the home, the use of Pot Pourri, in the next chapter when discussing flowers.

Our homes are an artificial extension of the earth we live upon. However, for many centuries, humans have built this extension using materials that naturally occur on or in the earth.

We have already seen how natural building materials enable houses to 'breathe' and are less likely to give off pollutant gases. The most worrisome indoor pollutant is probably formaldehyde gas. Levels of sensitivity vary from individual to individual, but repeated exposure to this substance can increase sensitivity and results in irritation of the mucous membranes of the eyes, nose and upper respiratory tract, headaches, lethargy, sleep disturbances, irritability, depression, etc. The greatest amount of this gas comes from products such as chipboard, urea-formaldehyde foam insulation and much contemporary furniture.

Lesser levels may be found in synthetic carpets, carpet glues, adhesives, oil-based paints and resins, plastics, ceiling tiles and through combustion (tobacco smoke, gas stoves, woodstoves and gas space heaters). Urea-formaldehyde resin can outgas (gradually releases gas) for the life of the product. Phenol-formaldehyde resin is less hazardous as it is more stable and is used in products such as exterior grade plywood. Because this is a difficult problem to deal with, particularly if you buy or rent a house which already contains such products, there is not a great deal you can do, although there are one or two houseplants you can use to absorb some of this gas (see chapter on Plants, Flowers & Crystals). If you feel that you may have such a sensitivity it may be possible to identify and replace the major sources. Good ventilation may also help alleviate the problem.

When buying new products for the home it is probably sensible, if you have any allergies, to buy those made from natural materials. However, not all natural products are free from allergic reactions. Be careful when buying softwoods as these give off a vapour which may trigger an allergic reaction in some people. Softwoods are pine, cedar, redwood and other conifers. Some people may even be allergic to Christmas Trees.

The materials we have used in the past to build our homes usually depended upon the area we lived in. Transport would have been difficult and expensive and only the wealthy could afford the luxury of using non-local materials. Stone, adobe (basically mud baked hard in the sun), cob (a mixture of mud and straw), bricks, plaster (made from lime), timber, thatch, grasses, cane and bamboo are all materials that have been used for centuries and are still available to us. Since the Industrial Revolution we also have metals and glass to use for construction. For indoor use we have a wide choice of natural fibres and fabrics such as wool, cotton, linen, silk, jute, hemp, sisal, rayon (based on cellulose derived from plant pulp), coir and hessian. Feathers and down, used as a traditional filling for bedding and cushions are lovely to use but some people may be allergic to these materials.

There is also a visual sense evoked by materials. High-tech metal 'feels' cold, and brick appears softer than concrete. Timber is universally warm, thick soft carpets have a luxurious feel, whilst rough sawn wood is rustic. Sheer fabrics in drapes evoke a sense of delicateness and lightness whilst velvet is soft but heavier and more imposing.

We also need to look at the types of paints and varnishes we use. Synthetic paints, varnishes and thinner solvents all contain volatile organic compounds as well as possibly toxic heavy metals. Lead used to be a common additive but is banned in the UK, USA and Australia. It is now possible to buy natural paints and varnishes which have subtle colouring and a pleasant fragrance and are derived from natural plant and mineral ingredients. Pigments are made from roots, bark, leaves, stems, flowers and fruit. Plants also oblige with resins, oils, starches and waxes that may be used as a thinning medium. Natural varnishes combine resins with scented turpentine oil, pigments and pure beeswax giving a golden lustre to all types of interior wood surfaces.

The earth on which we live can sustain us and still provide us with natural materials that can enhance and enrich our lives if we are willing to use our imaginations coupled with ideas from the past.

In the Chapter about Earth Energies, we saw how the earth's own energy system had areas of positive, negative and neutral energy which occurs naturally. Animals are intuitively aware of these areas and some animals have an affinity for positive areas and some for negative. It is possible that people have the same affinities. As we have seen we are a moving, oscillating ball of energy that vibrates at certain frequencies and each one of us is different - we have our very own electrical signature. Some of us will be happy and healthy living in a positive energy area, others may be just as happy and healthy living in a naturally negative energy area. However, it may be possible that in our modern world we have polluted our electromagnetic environment, causing many of us to become sensitive, even allergic, to a particular type of earth energy. Maybe there are some areas on the earth where humans do not thrive and in previous times we would probably have been aware enough never to have chosen to live there.

For the past five years in Germany there have been many studies on this subject which has become known as 'Geopathic Stress'. These studies have shown that people who live above certain types of underground water courses may have health problems. The energy does not seem to be compatible with the human energy system. Considerable research is still being done in Germany and Switzerland on the effects, causes and types of geopathic stress and earth energies.

People begin to suspect they have such a problem when they suffer from sleep disturbances and are ill only when at home (although this is far from the only reason). Sometimes they find relief from the problem by simply moving the bed into another part of the room or into a different room. Some researchers have developed devices that are designed to offset these effects, although one of the traditional remedies is to drive a copper or iron rod into the offending zone. It may be however, that this only diverts the effect to another area and much research still needs to be carried out on this subject.

In the United Kingdom we live in a temperate climate that is fairly variable in temperature. There are times when we need to heat our homes.

Temperature is something we only think about when it falls or rises to uncomfortable levels. The average person has a comfort zone of between 20°C (68°F) and 27°C (80°F) with 30% to 60% humidity when the air is still. We may be uncomfortable even within these tolerances if the air is too still, when we feel stifled or when there is a draught. However, if we modify our thermal environment to create a thermally stress-free zone, we may find that we lose our ability to sense the world around us as it has become too bland for our nervous systems. We are not meant to live in, and have not evolved in, a static environment.

People living in solar heated houses have suggested that it gives a new awareness and another dimension to their lives, with the sun taking on a greater importance.

We also have a stressful situation when we live in hot centrally heated houses and then enter the outdoor cold air. This is a shock to our system. Similarly those who live in air-conditioned environments may be shocked by high outdoor temperatures.

Ideally we need to keep indoor and outdoor temperatures more equalised.

Modern day furnaces and boilers are often hidden and so we lose our symbolic connections with the element of fire. We have already discussed the symbolic meaning of the hearth and the pleasure we derive from gazing at flames and embers. However wood is no longer considered such a suitable fuel for providing our heat as it may be difficult (although not impossible) to provide enough for everyone. The burning of wood in an open fire also produces pollution, however this may be reduced by using a modern high performance stove although not everyone has a fireplace or somewhere to put a wood burning stove.

Gas and oil are other possible fuel sources each with their own disadvantages, as those allergic to gas emissions know to their cost.

With all forms of non-renewable fuel we obviously have to consider energy conservation. This can be carried out as a gradual process and all we need is a bit of common sense as we need to balance energy conservation with our need for ventilation. We also need to develop sources of sustainable energies and may look to the other elements such as air which would provide us with wind power, or water for wave power. One of the most direct forms of energy, however, is from the fire of the sun and in the future most of our needs may be met by forms of solar power.

Electricity is often claimed to be the cleanest and most efficient form of energy but this does depend on how and where it is produced. It does, however, appear to be the cleanest form once it has arrived at the home.

We are so dependent upon electricity to heat and power our homes that we can barely imagine life without it. Unfortunately it is possible that this relatively new technology may have potentially harmful side-effects. It is becoming more well known that there may be problems associated with living too near high-tension power lines, but it is possible that there are also problems associated with the electricity we use within our homes.

It could be that electricity causes physical and psychological disturbances to our biological systems, but research into this area is still new and no-one is really sure what effects the common usage of electricity is having.

The earth has its own electromagnetic field that pulses at 7.83 Hz. Our own bioelectrical system pulses at about the same rate. This natural beat of the earth, known as Schumann Waves, is thought to be essential for our well-being. It may be possible that the widespread use of electricity at 50 Hz in the home may be masking this pulse. Our bodies are geared to the background levels of radiation and electromagnetic energies from the earth, sun and planets, and are sensitive to any unusual changes in those levels. Too much radiation is what usually worries us, but it has been shown that if all natural radiation is shielded from us we also suffer. It seems that certain types of building construction may act like a Faraday Cage which excludes all radiation causing us to suffer deprivation.

We also need to be aware of the various forms of static electricity and radiation emitted by colour televisions, VDU's and the possible side effects from defective microwave ovens.

The subtle energy field of the body is also affected by sympathetic resonance with similar force fields. Notice how we can be affected by the presence of other people on a day to day basis and how moods can take over a crowd or a room full of people. This is called Bio-entrainment and due to this effect, we might possibly become 'addicted' to having our energies disharmonised by the use of electronic equipment, computers and televisions. This may be why those who appear to be 'addicted' to television or computer video games, experience an energy depletion.

We live in a sea of electromagnetic energies and we need to bear in mind that we too are electrical beings, and can be affected by the uses we make of electricity and electromagnetic fields, such as those emitted by the mains supply alternating current pulsating at 50 or 60 Hz.

The element of water is fundamental to life, a vital sustainer that is very much a part of our bodies as well as covering a large proportion of the planet. Although the surface of the earth is mainly covered by water, most of this is salt water or ice. Only 1% is available as fresh water and nearly all life on this planet depends upon this 1%. Interestingly, it is thought that as much as one quarter of the world's fresh water is contained in Lake Baykal in Russia.

Water is a remarkable substance. Lyall Watson in the book *Supernature*, explains how it may be possible for cosmic activity to affect a living being because water makes up such a large part of the body (in humans the figure is 65%). Water is a chemical compound of the two elements, hydrogen and oxygen, H_2O. It is one of the very few substances that is denser in its liquid state than in its solid state, ie ice. This is important for all life on earth as this means that ice floats on water. Were this not so, as the oceans and lakes froze, the ice would sink to the bottom exposing the next 'layer' of water, which would freeze and sink, thus 'locking up' the world's water for ever.

The way that the atoms of hydrogen and oxygen join is by a weak chemical bond, being only 10% the strength of most chemical bonds, so there have to be a lot of bonds to keep it together. As ice, it forms the most perfectly bonded hydrogen structure known. So precise is this crystalline pattern that it seems to persist into the liquid state, and whilst remaining clear, water contains areas of ice crystals that form and melt many millions of times per second. In effect water seems to remember the form of ice by repeating the formula frequently to itself, being ready to change back into ice at any time.

Water then is amazingly flexible and also appears to be able to be imprinted with, and remember, different vibrational patterns. This is why it is used as a base for Flower Essences/Remedies and some homeopathic remedies, etc.

One remarkable man, Viktor Schauberger, born in Austria in 1885, became very knowledgeable about water. He was a 'true son of the forest' as his family had almost exclusively interested themselves in the husbandry of the forests. He was apprenticed to an old forest warden and eventually, due to his ideas and applications in connection with log flumes, became State Consultant for Timber Flotation Installations. He was later employed by one of Austria's largest building contractors and built many log flumes in Austria and elsewhere in Europe. Throughout his years of closeness with nature and his work, Schauberger built up a vast store of knowledge about water and became aware that the most beneficial was what could be described as Living Water.

Living water is water that has completed a full cycle from the earth to the atmosphere and back again, where according to Schauberger adequate vegetation cover allows rainwater to penetrate quite deeply, sinking by cooling until the weight of water above equals the pressure of the deeply drained water below. This latter heated by the earth rises due to having a lower specific weight. Apparently this warmer water is involved in a carbon hydrogen and oxygen reaction that enables it to 'pick up' minerals and salts which it brings towards the surface as nutrients for vegetation.

Schauberger did not approve of pumped sub-surface water as drinking water as he believed it to be 'immature' and had not passed through the whole of its natural cycle. Only the water that runs out from the soil by itself in the form of springs and streams was considered suitable.

Spring water, particularly mountain spring water, contains a relatively high content of carbon matter. As it descends from the mountains it flows in a certain motion - meandering and swirling, forming vortexes, and flowing in a very organic manner. This motion can be duplicated artificially and is called a 'cycloid spiral motion'.

John Wilkes, artist and sculptor, was inspired by the moving qualities of natural water and in 1970 started experimenting with water sculptures. These he called 'flow form vessels' which induces the rhythmically swinging motion of water streaming down a mountain which energies and vitalises the water. There is now a flow form vessel in the famous Chalice Well Garden at Glastonbury in Somerset. These flow forms are also being studied in relation to natural filtration systems which make use of such things as reedbeds. The flow forms are the final stage of the process.

The healing properties of water have long been valued and natural springs with their unique mineral content have become the focal point of spas and resorts around the world. The Greeks and Romans were firm believers in the therapeutic effects of hot springs. The Japanese have also utilised the healing benefits by using natural springs and hot tubs in the home, and in the western world Jacuzzis are gaining favour.

The major threat to our water nowadays is contamination. Industrial waste dumping, landfill, radioactive wastes, agricultural pesticides and fertilisers, and leaking septic tanks, all percolate into rivers, lakes and groundwater. Added to that is the airborne pollution of the atmosphere which mixes with the moisture in the air to form acid rain. It is everyone's personal responsibility to ensure that toxic household and garden products are not added to the water system. Sewage treatment plants are not equipped to deal with such pollutants and many will eventually be passed back into our drinking water supplies.

There are many home water filtration systems available, ranging from the jug type filter to the 'point of use' systems that use either activated carbon, reverse osmosis or distillation principles.

There is also a wide range of bottled water to choose from if you are concerned about the quality of your drinking water.

We also need to be aware of the importance of water in our lives and not waste it unnecessarily. In North America the average family of four can use an average of up to 220 gallons (1000 litres) per day which is between two and four times the average consumption for a European family.

New, and more efficient toilets, washing machines and dishwashers are being developed which should help but we can also contribute by not using drinking quality water for tasks such as washing the car or watering the garden. Collect rainwater or recycle waste water to use for these purposes, and water gardens with watering cans instead of hoses and cover soil with a mulch of compost or bark chippings to reduce evaporation and thus reduce the need for watering.

Water is of such great importance to us that we need to redevelop the sense of sacredness our ancestors had about water.

Springs and wells were considered so special that they often had their own guardian spirit or healing lady associated with them. To the Celts, springs and wells were the entrances to the mysterious underworld, a potent realm of power where life and death originated.

One of the most famous springs is located in the beautiful city of Bath in England. Even before the Romans built their baths, the inhabitants had held the hot springs in reverence. The Latin name Aquae Sulis, means literally 'the waters of the goddess of the gap'. Perhaps in our modern and 'enlightened' times we would do well to remember and respect the sacredness of this very special substance.

CHAPTER 9

PLANTS, FLOWERS AND CRYSTALS

Now that we have looked at the basics we can turn our attention to what some of us may think of as embellishments. We do not appear to need these things for our survival on a physical level and yet in our ordinary day to day life our emotional and spiritual needs require nourishment.

Given the possibility of such a strong connection on the subtle energy levels between our emotions and the physical body, we would do well to consider the more intangible needs for our well-being.

The ancient Chinese had a saying, to the effect that, if you have only a small amount of money, use half to buy bread and half to buy flowers. They clearly understood that flowers nourish the spirit in the same way that bread nourishes the body.

We need things in our home that connect us with our external environment, to the rhythms of nature, and which have symbolic meaning for us universally, culturally or personally. This will help lead us toward wholeness.

One of the most potent of these 'things' is plants, which fulfil all of the above criteria because they are part of the living earth itself and cannot be considered as just objects. On some level they interact with us, and whilst we give them a home, they give us untold benefits.

Our relationship with houseplants can provide a powerful connection with life and with the planet. They change and respond to their own rhythms, planetary cycles and to the care we give them. There are also beneficial side effects for those of us who care for plants. They depend upon us to survive and therefore we feel we are needed, and since humanity has a long history of working with plants we generally find that caring for them is therapeutic. So much so that a form of Horticultural Therapy has been developed and is used in helping to treat a wide range of physical and mental disabilities.

Plants and soil also make a perfect ecological air purifying system. They filter and purify the air by sedimentation and absorption. Using a process known as photosynthesis, plants convert sunlight into energy, absorb carbon dioxide in the air and replace it with oxygen. By transpiration through leaves and drinking via roots, they also help to regulate the humidity, modify temperatures and balance the ions in the air.

At NASA, the space research scientists were surprised to discover that certain plants are also excellent absorbers of some pollutants. One of the most common pollutants, formaldehyde, is absorbed efficiently by the Spider Plant (Chlorophytum comosun). Other plants found to be suitable for this purpose were the Mother-in-Law's Tongue (Sansevieria trifasciata,) Philodendrons, Dracaena and Chrysanthemums. Researchers at Reading University have also discovered that under certain conditions, plants with high photosynthesis rates, such as Hibiscus and Fiscus elastica (Rubber Plant) can dramatically reduce the levels of carbon dioxide present and also have an influence on humidity and temperature levels. Research undertaken in both Britain and Switzerland has shown that the cactus Cereus peruvianus is capable of absorbing electromagnetic emissions given off from VDU's and colour televisions.

We have already seen how plants respond to sound and music. It has also been suggested by some researchers that plants are more aware than we realise and they are capable of knowing what we are doing, and even thinking, and can respond to the emotions being generated by someone they form a relationship with. Those interested in this fascinating subject would enjoy reading *The Secret Life of Plants*' by Peter Tompkins and Christopher Bird. They describe how in 1966, America's foremost lie-detector examiner, Cleve Backster, started investigating our relationship with plants. He used a Dracaena, a tropical plant with large leaves and a dense cluster of small flowers, and attached to one of its leaves the electrodes of his lie-detector. He then poured water onto its roots and was surprised to find that the tracing showed a similar reaction to that of a human being experiencing a brief emotional stimulus.

Further experiments showed that the plant reacted not only to actual harm but even to the threat of physical harm. In one experiment Backster had intended to burn one of the leaves, but found that the plant reacted at the time he thought of doing so. If a plant was threatened with overwhelming danger or damage, Backster observed that it appeared to 'pass out' rather in the way a human would.

This is interesting in view of the method used by some native American Indian tribes to cut down a tree for their Totem Pole. The men would rush toward their chosen tree, noisily informing it that it was going to be cut down. After several minutes they would then cut down another tree and use this for their Totem Pole. The idea seemed to be that the threat was enough to make all the trees in the vicinity faint so that the cutting of the tree would not be so distressing for it, or the surrounding trees.

After a series of observations Backster noticed that a special bond of affinity seemed to be created between a plant and its keeper, even when they were not in close proximity. It appears that once attuned to a particular person, plants are able to maintain a link with that person even at a distance.

It is well known that some people are blessed with a 'green thumb' - the ability to help plants thrive, and that others have the opposite effect as their plants always appear to die no matter how carefully they tend them.

This could be related to differences on a vibrational or electrical level or could be related to how the plants perceive people. Talking to your plant may not be as 'way out' as some people imagine, and I am convinced that plants respond on some level to the way we act toward them.

Indoors is an alien environment for plants which have often originated in tropical countries and their survival is totally dependant upon you and the way you treat them. Different types of plants need particular levels of light and exposure to the sun and the correct amount of water and food. You cannot place a plant just anywhere for a decorative effect, you have to become aware of its needs and its likes and dislikes.

When you buy a plant there will usually be a card that gives you the information you need, such as whether it prefers direct sunlight, non-direct light, or a degree of shade, how often it requires watering and what, and when, to feed it. These are guidelines and you may find you need to make adjustments depending on your personal environment. Also bear in mind the plants ultimate size.

Plants often look good grouped together, this also helps the plants by creating a mini eco-climate around them. They usually like around 60% humidity whereas our living rooms are usually about 20%. When plants are grouped together you could place them on a large tray covered with pebbles which you can keep moist - this will help to increase the humidity around the plants. You could also use a mist-sprayer for this purpose.

Plants vary in shape, leaf shape, texture and colour but are predominately a vibrant living green that goes well with any colour scheme. They even improve your social life as it has been shown that people relax and linger in room full of plants.

Many plants also produce beautiful flowers which are an extra bonus, adding colour, and sometimes fragrance, to a room.

Flowers represent the highest pinnacle of the plant's life because they have the function of continuing the life of the plant that bears them. They are often portrayed in poetry and art as symbols of perfection or as having spiritual qualities.

An inspired horticulturist, George Washington Carver, once said:

> *"When I touch that flower, I am touching infinity. It existed long before there were human beings on this earth and will continue to exist for millions of years to come. Through the flower, I talk to the Infinite, which is only a silent force. This is not a physical contact. It is not the earthquake, wind or fire. It is in the invisible world."*

Many years ago I came across a beautiful poem by Nikos Kazantzakis:

I said to the almond tree "Sister speak to me of God" And the almond tree blossomed.

The Greeks and Romans were almost obsessive about flowers and their banqueting halls were decorated with incredible quantities of flowers which were thought to stimulate the appetite of the guests. The Greek nymph of flowers was called Chloris and the Romans worshipped the goddess Flora, celebrating the festival of Floralia in her honour, usually in May.

Flowers seem to have been connected with the ancient concepts of the after-life, for even in the gloomy regions of the Elysian Fields, presided over by Pluto, God of the Underworld, the plains were covered with flowers.

Flowers were also put on graves by the Greeks and Romans to symbolise eternal life. Originally funeral flowers represented a floral offering or even a token sacrifice to the departed with a view to reconciling them to their fate and the funeral wreath was possibly no more than a magic circle designed to enclose the dead soul.

The ancient Egyptians even crowned their dead with chaplets of flowers. Floral wreaths were strongly opposed by the early Christian church because of their pagan associations, but the magic of flowers proved to be stronger and wreaths have continued to be used.

The greatest loved of all flowers has to be the rose. To the ancient Greeks the rose was the emblem of Venus. In the language of flowers the red rose represents love and the white rose silence. Together they symbolise unity. Roman brides wore garlands of roses on their wedding day and it was probably the Romans who first brought roses to Britain. Roses were also highly valued for their medicinal qualities.

During the Victorian era, the language of flowers became very widespread, each flower in a bouquet having a specific meaning. Dictionaries of this language became very popular and one could express devotion, passion, jealousy and a whole range of emotions through the use of bouquets or cards portraying the appropriate blossoms.

A graceful flower arrangement is one of the most delightful ways to bring flowers into your home. The arrangement may be as simple or as complex as you desire. One flower in a glass bowl can be as eloquent as a mass of arranged flowers. You can artistically arrange for shape and form, colour, texture and fragrance and each time you look appreciatively at a flower I like to think that the plants and inherent intelligences within them, feel and respond to your appreciation.

I think it is possible that many people have an instinctive appreciation of the intelligence within plants and throughout history there has been reference to some sort of link between humans and nature.

In Japan the early Buddhist Monks, who revered the sacredness of all life, would gather the flowers and twigs that lay on the ground after a storm. Thus the art of Ikebana was born and historically it was considered men's work, studied even by the Samurai Warriors. This ancient art is taught from childhood, like painting and sculpture, and gives everyone a chance to express a love of nature. There are many styles of Ikebana and each has specific requirements as to the placement of every branch and flower, the design, colour relationships and the containers used.

When gathering flowers for arrangements the best time is early morning before the sun rises or late afternoon when they are at their peak. Bear in mind that the cutting of a flower is a form of pruning which increases the plant's ability to produce more flowers, even so I would always say a thank you. As a guideline, only gather flowers where they are in abundance and try to leave some on the plant. In the case of wild flowers, do not pick these indiscriminately as it is illegal to pick certain species.

Always use a sharp tool and cut the stalk cleanly, picking some in flower and some in bud. Put into a jar or bucket of water immediately after cutting, and it will not harm them if you need to leave them in the container for a few hours. Before you arrange them, recut the stems at an angle so they can absorb more water. Those flowers with woody stems, such as lilacs, benefit from having their stems gently hammered to split the ends. Flowers, like poppies, whose stems have a milky sap, can be lightly burnt with a match to seal them. Remove submerged leaves and change the water every few days. Keep the arrangement out of direct sunlight as much as possible.

Whilst dried flowers may not be as evocative as fresh flowers, they do serve to brighten up our days when fresh flowers are out of season, unavailable, or unaffordable. The drying of flowers alters their colour and texture which makes them more rigid and static when you come to arrange them. They can be mixed with other plant materials such as grasses and eucalyptus and effective arrangements can be created on a theme, such as the use of one colour or a mass of one particular flower.

The easiest way to dry flowers is to hang them in a bunch upside down in a cool, airy place. Remove leaves prior to drying and do not put too many flowers in one bunch. Many flowers hold their shape and colour well when dried this way, for example, the everlastings - strawflowers, statice and globe amaranth, globe thistles, baby's breath, hydrangea, lavender and sea holly. Pick the flowers on a warm, dry day to avoid moisture which may lead to mould.

There are other methods using desiccants such as sand, silica gel and borax. There are many books available on this subject or you may wish to buy the finished product. One of the best places to find a wide range of dried flower arrangements is a good quality craft fair.

Another way to use flowers so that they give lasting pleasure, with the added bonus of fragrance, is to make, or buy, Pot Pourri. Pot Pourri is translated from the French 'rotten pot' because of the traditional moist methods of making it where the ingredients literally do rot. It is more common nowadays, however, to make, or buy those made by the dry method. Pot Pourri is made from three main ingredient - flowers and herbs, essential oils and a fixative of some kind to preserve the fragrance and petals. Fragrant fruit rinds and spices such as cloves and cinnamon can also be added for scent, colour and texture. The most common fixatives are Calamus Root from the Sweet Flag, Gum Benzoin, a resinous gum from the Indonesian tree Styrax, and Orrisroot, the rootstock of the Florentine Iris which has its own violet-like scent.

The flowers can be dried whole or as individual petals by spreading them in a thin layer on wicker trays or screens. These are placed in a warm dark place to dry. Shake them daily and keep covered with a piece of cheesecloth to keep off the dust. When the flowers or petals are totally dry keep them in air-tight containers until you are ready to use them.

Prepare the Pot Pourri by combining dried flowers, herbs, and if used, fruit rinds and a selection of spices in a large bowl, gently mixing them together. Add a small amount (one or two drops to begin with) of essential oil until the right fragrance is achieved. Then add the powdered fixative and mix thoroughly. Put the mixture away in a sealed container in a warm, dry area for six weeks to cure. When the Pot Pourri is ready display it in an open bowl or container of your choice and decorate the top with a few whole flower heads to add final colour.

Pot Pourri made from the flowers and herbs grown in your own garden is a delightful way to maintain your link to this beautiful aspect of nature.

Crystals could be considered the flowers of the mineral world and whilst they may not appear to have the same sort of living presence as plants and flowers, they provide a tangible link to our connection with the mineral kingdom. To my mind they are 'alive', after all, crystals grow.

There are many beautiful crystals but the ones I find most evocative and generally beneficial in the home, are quartz crystals. The importance of crystals, and in particular quartz, has been recognised through many civilisations. Legends and myths abound with their use, for magic, divination and healing, and many cultures have been aware of their sacredness and life-enhancing potential. Clear quartz crystal, called the Stone of Power, or the Living Stone, has symbolised truth, clarity and light throughout the ages, and today many people are recognising its value both as a healing and meta-physical tool.

Quartz crystal has an incredibly organised atomic structure with very stable oscillations, so stable that other oscillations in the vicinity tend to synchronise with the Quartz. Because of this quartz crystal appears to have the ability to bring into balance unsynchronised or unbalanced energies. This gives a generally mellowing effect on the immediate environment and if you spend time with these beautiful crystals you may begin to notice a balancing out of any discordant energies. It appears that we begin to resonate in harmony with these stable structures whose natural frequencies are of a harmonious nature.

There are many different types of quartz but the ones I use for a generally therapeutic effect in the home are clear quartz, either singly or doubly terminated points, spheres or clusters (clusters are a cluster of single points that are still attached to the rock matrix). I also use Amethyst, the beautiful violet quartz found in abundance in Brazil, again in clusters or single points and Rose Quartz which does not generally form points but is available in chunks in a rough or polished form and is a lovely pink colour with a calm and gentle energy.

It has been suggested that quartz crystals, particularly in the form of clusters, have an ionising effect on the air, bringing the balance of positive and negative ions into the right ratio.

Clear crystals can be placed around the room or put with plants for their mutual benefit. Amethyst creates the right ambience for meditation and contemplation as well as being very decorative, and rose quartz is useful for helping you to release negative emotions such as anger and fear.

Crystals, like plants, need a certain amount of care. They like to be cleansed in running water for a couple of minutes and put outdoors in sunlight occasionally. If the subject is of interest to you I have written a book called *Crystal Clear - A Guide to Quartz Crystal*, published by Capall Bann, which will give you a basic understanding.

There are of course a vast range of crystals and minerals, many of which are highly decorative, have beautiful colours, as well as being of value in a healing context. If you have the chance to choose from such a range I suggest you choose those which 'catch your eye' and really appeal to you, as that particular stone is probably resonating on your frequency.

Plants, flowers and crystals are an intrinsic part of my home and I cannot imagine home without them. They connect me to nature, to the earth, to my roots and thus to my spiritual self, and I hope that in the future we will continue to use them in our homes. I was very pleased to see, when watching Star Trek, The Next Generation, that the Crew Quarters on the Starship Enterprise were decorated with beautiful plants, flowers and crystals. Live Long and Prosper!

CHAPTER 10

HEALING IN THE HOME

In the previous chapters we have discussed how certain aspects of our homes can be arranged to create a healing environment. In this Chapter I want to suggest safe and simple methods of healing that can be used for minor conditions. Apart from the sensible proven methods of general first aid and the provision of pain killers, cough medicine and patent remedies, there are valuable, effective, but not so well known methods of healing that can be utilised by anyone in their own home.

These methods have their roots in nature and are generally simple rather than complex. However, the way some of them work may be new to many because they work on what is called the vibrational level - the level of energy inherent within form. In Chapter 1 we looked at the suggested existence of subtle energy fields which underlie physical existence and reality. Vibrational healing, as its name suggests, aims to treat imbalance whilst it still exists in the subtle energy field, or, because it may be difficult to detect the problem at this level, to treat the physical body by attempting to bring the subtle energies back into balance.

Colour Therapy and Sound or Music Therapy are considered to be forms of vibrational healing but to actively treat conditions of imbalance with colour or sound one needs to undergo a recognised form of training. It is, of course, possible for anyone to learn the basics about colour and sound and utilise them in everyday living, but there are also some simple vibrational therapies that are so safe that it is possible for anyone to learn to use them, for themselves, or for their family.

We have already looked at the benefits of having plants, flowers and crystals in our homes, but these 'substances' can be utilised in certain vibrational therapies which are simple to use. Probably the most well known of these is Homeopathy. Again this is a complete system of therapy requiring extensive training if it is to be used to treat medical conditions. However, it is possible to use some homeopathic remedies safely for self-care and first aid in the home. The fact that homeopathic remedies are without side effects and are safe even for small children makes them eminently suitable for self-medication in the treatment of minor ailments. As always, where any symptoms persist beyond a reasonable period you should consult your doctor.

Homeopathy today is practised by qualified practitioners worldwide and has become recognised over the years as an effective and inherently safe form of medical treatment. In Britain it has been favoured by various members of the Royal Family and is recognised by Act of Parliament and all homeopathic medicines are available on prescription under the National Health Service.

So what exactly is Homeopathy? The word is derived from the Greek "Homoios" meaning 'like' and 'pathos' meaning 'suffering'. The basic principle of this system has been known since the time of the ancient Greeks. This principle is the practice of treating like with like. In effect this means treating an illness with a substance which when taken by a healthy person produces symptoms similar to those displayed by the person who is ill. Homeopathy sees the symptoms as the body's reaction against illness as it attempts to recover, and so seeks to stimulate and not suppress the reaction. Current medical opinion says that symptoms are the direct manifestation of an illness, and seek to cure by suppressing the symptoms.

Present day homeopathic methods were developed in the 18th Century by Dr. Samuel Hahnemann, a German physician, who was so appalled by the medical practices of the day, that he sought a method of healing which would be safe, gentle and effective. His basic belief was that human beings have the ability to heal themselves and that the symptoms shown reflect the individual's attempt to overcome the illness. Dr. Hahnemann reasoned that it might be more beneficial to stimulate a symptom and so encourage the body's natural healing process.

This reasoning was supported when he took an infusion of quinine (cinchona bark) which produced the symptoms of Malaria. When the quinine was given to a patient suffering from Malaria it alleviated the symptoms.

Hahnemann further discovered that remedies obtained from animal, vegetable and mineral sources were effective and over a long period he, and his assistants, took small doses of various substances, carefully noting the symptoms they produced. These were called 'provings'. Hahnemann then worked to establish the smallest effective dose. In doing so he unexpectedly discovered the second principle of homeopathy -

that the more a remedy is diluted, the more effective it becomes. This method of dilution also allowed substances which were poisonous at full strength, to be used with no side effects. This finding became known as the Law of Potencies and unfortunately proved to be one of the greatest stumbling blocks to the new system. Many people, and the medical establishment in particular, found it impossible to believe that such tiny amounts, diluted over and over again, could have any effect on the patient. Despite this scepticism, however, Hahnemann eventually became an internationally respected figure and homeopathy was well established in many countries before his death. Hahnemann himself was not sure how the thoroughly diluted substances actually worked - he only knew that they did.

The third principle of homeopathy is that people vary in their response to illness, according to their basic temperament, thus homeopathy concentrates on treating the patient rather than the disease.

If we go back to the possibilities offered by the framework of subtle energies we can see how it may be possible for the diluted substances to have a direct effect even when there is no measurable chemical content left after such profound dilution. What appears to be left is the vibrational frequency of the substance used. This vibrational frequency seems to be released by the process of dilution which traditionally involves the use of water and the action of very thorough shaking called 'succussion'. It has been suggested that the shaking action could have the effect of releasing the vibration of the substance into the water and that water, as we have previously seen, is a most remarkable substance that may have the ability to 'remember'.

Conventional science has never accepted the possibility that water can 'remember' the vibrational frequencies of other substances, and has recently been disconcerted by the work of a French scientist, Jacques Benveniste who rocked the medical world with laboratory evidence that drugs worked in the micro-dilutions used by homeopathy. Benveniste has since been repudiated by the Scientific community, and his laboratory at the French National Medical Research Organisation has been closed. Such was the offence caused to mainstream science that the scientific journal Nature conducted an independent investigation of the work. This investigation was carried out on behalf of Nature by a writer on scientific fraud and a stage magician turned psychic investigator! This goes to show that proof of the simple fact that water has the ability to remember, would upset the findings of current scientific thought. However, Tony Pinkus, Homeopathic pharmacist to the British Royal Family is quoted as saying in the Sept/Oct 1994 Issue of *Mind Body & Soul*:

> *What is new and really significant is the growing realisation that the action of homeopathic remedies is far removed from chemistry, and happens in the domain of physics, and specifically quantum physics.*

Despite all argument however, we just need to remember that this system of healing has shown itself to be very beneficial.

The homeopathic medicines in common use are stocked in most health stores and many chemists and I suggest that if this method of healing is of interest, that you purchase the booklet called *"Homeopathy for the Family"* available from such shops. This inexpensive and invaluable booklet is published by Wigmore Publications Ltd and is recommended by the Homeopathic Development Foundation Ltd. It lists the 38 medicines in common use and gives suggestions for their use, an Index of Symptoms and a Guide to the Selection of Medicines plus a list of medicines and their Indications (what they can be used for).

Many plant and mineral substances are utilised in homeopathy and are constantly being extended as leading homeopathic researchers develop and test new ideas such as the use of hydrogen, chocolate, and poison from the sting of a scorpion.

Another vibrational therapy also utilises the concept of releasing the vibrational frequency or energy of a substance into water and was also developed by a doctor who worked for many years in conventional medicine and homeopathy. This therapy is known as the Bach Flower Remedies, developed by Dr. Edward Bach (pronounced Batch). Again, discouraged by the methods of traditional medicine, Dr. Bach desired to develop a form of healing that was gentle and safe. He also realised that it was necessary to treat the patient and not the disease and in 1930 he gave up his lucrative practice and research to devote his time to the finding of 'The Remedies' and perfecting this method of Flower Healing.

These remedies are prescribed, not for a physical complaint, but according to the patients' emotional state of mind, depending upon their various moods such as fear, worry, anger or depression. It is well known that a long continued fear or worry will deplete an individual's vitality and affect their immune system which may lose its natural resistance to disease. Dr. Bach developed thirty eight remedies, one for each of the most common negative states of mind. These remedies were taken from the flowers of wild plants and trees, and one even taken from the living water.

It was Dr. Bach's intention that these remedies could be used by anyone, even in their own home, as they are totally benign in their action and can never produce an unpleasant reaction under any condition.

He divided the negative states of mind into seven groups - fear, uncertainty, insufficient interest in present circumstances, loneliness, over-sensitivity to influences and ideas, despondency or despair, and overcare for the welfare of others.

The following list in alphabetical order is intended to give a general indication of the state of mind and the plant used:

Agrimony:	Those who hide worries behind a brave face.
Aspen:	Apprehension for no known reason.
Beech:	Critical and intolerant of others.
Centaury:	Weak willed, exploited or imposed upon.
Cerato:	Those who doubt their own judgement.
Cherry Plum:	Uncontrolled irrational thoughts.
Chestnut Bud:	Refuses to learn by experience.
Chicory:	Over possessive and self-centred.
Clematis:	Inattentive, dreamy and absent-minded.
Crab Apple:	The 'Cleanser', Self disgust.
Elm:	Overwhelmed by inadequacy and responsibility.
Gentian:	Despondency.
Gorse:	Pessimism, Defeatism.
Heather:	Talkative, obsessed with own troubles.
Holly:	Hatred, Envy, Jealousy and Suspicion.
Honeysuckle:	Living in the past, Home-sickness.
Hornbeam:	'Monday morning' feeling, Procrastination.
Impatiens:	Impatience, irritability.
Larch:	Lack of self-confidence, fears failure.
Mimulus:	Fear of known things, shyness.
Mustard:	'Dark Cloud' that descends for no reason.
Oak:	Normally strong, but no longer able to cope.
Olive:	Fatigued and drained of energy.
Pine:	Guilt Complex, always apologising.
Red Chestnut:	Obsessed by care and concern for others.
Rock Rose:	Suddenly alarmed, scared and panicky.
Rock Water:	Rigid minded, self denying.
Scleranthus:	Uncertainty/indecision.
Star of Bethlehem:	For all effects of serious news.
Sweet Chestnut:	Utter dejection, bleak outlook.
Vervain:	Over-enthusiasm, fanatical beliefs.
Vine:	Dominating, inflexible, tyrannical, arrogant.
Walnut:	Assists in adjustment or change.
Water Violet:	Proud, reserved, enjoys being alone.
White Chestnut:	Persistent unwanted thoughts.
Wild Oat:	Helps determine one's intended path in life.
Wild Rose:	Resignation, apathy.
Willow:	Resentment, embitterment.

There is also a Combination Remedy consisting of Cherry Plum, Clematis, Impatiens, Rock Rose and Star of Bethlehem which is called Rescue Remedy and this is considered to be an all purpose emergency remedy for the effects of anguish, examinations, going to the dentist, etc., and this is a remedy I have used on numerous occasions for people, animals and plants, particularly when overstressed or in a state of shock.

These remedies are readily available at most Health Stores or Alternative shops and have directions for use on the bottle. There is also an information leaflet available which gives more detailed directions. If you cannot find a local stockist I have given the address of the Bach Centre, where Dr. Bach lived and worked until his death, at the end of the book.

The method of making flower remedies, devised by Dr. Bach, possibly from more ancient methods, consists of placing the flowers onto pure water that is contained in a thin glass bowl. Sufficient flowers are picked and floated on the water so as to cover the surface. This must be done on a clear sunny day when there are no clouds and the flowers are in perfect bloom. The bowl is then left in sunlight for 3-4 hours. By a process of natural alchemy the energy of the flower is transferred to the water. The flowers are then removed and the liquid is poured into bottles with an equal volume of brandy which acts as a preservative. A few of the remedies cannot be prepared in this way and are made by the 'boiling method'. The selected parts of the plant are boiled for 30 minutes in pure water, strained off and the liquid is preserved with brandy as before.

This extract, by either method, is called the 'essence' sometimes referred to as the 'mother tincture'. Two drops of the essence are sufficient to potentise a one ounce bottle of brandy and this becomes a stock bottle of that particular remedy. This stock bottle is what is purchased and can be further diluted in water when taken. It is possible to take up to five remedies together without impairing their effect.

In the last ten years or so, many developments have been made utilising this method of releasing the vibrational energy from different substances, mostly flowers, including tree and vegetable flowers and also from minerals, crystals and gems. The newer types of flower remedies are usually called Flower Essences to avoid confusion with the original Dr. Bach Flower Remedies, and those made from minerals are usually called Gem Remedies or Essences. We now have a range of Flower Essences such as the Californian, Alaskan, Perelandra (Virginian), Australian Bush, Amazon Orchid, Pacific, and Hawaiian Flower Essences, the Bailey Essences, Green Man Tree Essences and the Findhorn Flower Essences. These mostly work on emotional, psychological, mental or spiritual states of mind and greatly expand the states of mind suggested by Dr. Bach, as it is generally felt that since the 1930's humanity has had to deal with a whole range of psychological effects and stresses caused by the accelerated growth of the modern world.

As well as the Bach Flower Remedies, I have also worked with the Perelandra (Virginian) Flower Essences, which consist of eight Rose Essences and eighteen Garden Essences from the flowers of garden vegetables and herbs. These Flower Essences work directly with both the electrical and central nervous system in order to balance the electrical (subtle) system and stabilise the nervous system.

Gem Remedies or Essences are made from many different metals, minerals, gems and crystals and are also 'prescribed' for particular states of mind. They are said, however, to work a little more directly on the physical body although they still work through the subtle energies of the body.

The more recent Flower Essences and Gem Remedies are not quite so readily available and are more often to be found in 'alternative' or 'New Age' shops or by mail order directly from The Flower and Gem Remedy Association (address at back of book).

Aromatherapy, the use of essential oils, is another therapy that is used to treat a variety of conditions. A professionally qualified Aromatherapist will use a wide range of oils but there are a selection of essential oils that can be safely used in the home.

The most commonly available and safest essential oils, and their properties are as follows:

Lavender: Mildest but very effective essential oil. Appears to restore balance at all levels. Soothing, calms the emotions, alleviates headaches, excellent antiseptic.

Tea-tree: Powerful antiseptic, can be used as a disinfectant. Ideal for vapourising to kill germs.

Rosemary: Very stimulating oil, aids clear thinking. Good as a hair tonic and muscle rub, good for morning baths, is said to cleanse the subtle energy field. Do not use during pregnancy or if prone to high blood pressure or epilepsy.

Eucalyptus: Strong antiseptic, very penetrating aroma, useful for clearing the head during colds or can be used in massage oil as a clearing chest rub. Advisable to test for irritation if you have sensitive skin.

Peppermint: Used extensively for flavouring. Penetrating odour, invigorating. Lifts the spirits. Has a cooling effect in the body. Effective for tired and sweaty feet. Aids digestion. Advisable to test for irritation.

Jasmine: Very expensive in its concentrated form. Usually
                  available ready blended with Jojoba oil (more
                  wax-like than an oil and therefore has great
                  keeping qualities). This makes it affordable for
                  home use. Relaxing, alleviates stress, said to
                  unite apparent opposites. Sensual, heady floral
                  aroma. Do not use during pregnancy.

Rose: Very expensive, again often blended to be
                  affordable. Known as the Queen of Oils and the
                  flower of love. Good for females. Used in skin
                  care. Calms anger, facilitates creativity, sensual,
                  sweet floral aroma.

Neroli: Very expensive, again usually blended. Made
                  from the flowers of the bitter orange. Useful for
                  calming the emotions and relieving stress. Helps
                  restore sleep, very good for mature and dry skins.
                  Light floral aroma.

Ylang Ylang: 'Flower of Flowers' - a sweet and exotic oil often
                  used for its sensual properties. Calms negative
                  emotional states, soothing and soporific, good for
                  dry skins and as a hair rinse.

Geranium: A refreshing balancing oil for both mind and body.
                  Good for clearing congestion and to help eliminate
                  cellulite. Excellent for skin care. Very pleasing
                  flowery aroma. Good for fragrancing the home
                  and is a useful insect repellent.

Chamomile: Fairly expensive. Very good for sensitive or dry
                  skins. Relaxing aroma which has soothing
                  properties. Useful oil for children. Can be used
                  in shampoo to help lighten the hair.

Juniper: An antiseptic and astringent oil ideal for oily skins. A stimulating oil good for massage into scalp. Has a generally cleansing effect. Has diuretic qualities. Good for calming worried or anxious states of mind. Test skin for irritation.

Frankincense: Has a warm and soothing aroma, traditionally used as an aid to meditation. Very good for mature skins. Calms anxiety and tension, helps clear catarrh and other mucous conditions.

Sandalwood: Also used as an aid to meditation, this oil has a rich musky aroma. Again excellent for skin care. Helps dispel depression or tension.

Orange: A very uplifting oil. Good for fragrancing the room. Ideal at Christmas time.

Lemon: An excellent antiseptic, very refreshing and uplifting. Good as a hair rinse and can be used to lighten hands that are stained. Aids clear thinking. Note that citrus oils should not be used on skin when exposed to the sun and also test for irritation if you have a sensitive skin.

Falling part way between a vibrational and physical therapy, the essential oils themselves are diluted for use and possibly act in a subtle way on our energy fields as well as emotionally through our sense of smell and physically on the body.

As discussed in the Chapter on Air, essential oils are extremely concentrated liquids (feeling more like water than oil) that are extracted from flowers, leaves, roots, seeds, barks and resins and some of them are a useful addition to the remedies that can be used in the home.

For self help, essential oils are most commonly used to relieve aches and pains, for relaxation and stress reduction, and for skin and hair care. Many oils also have proven antiseptic properties and can be used for the on-going treatment of cuts, burns, insect bites and stings, and for bruises. Some are anti-inflammatory and/or antibacterial, and oils with anti-fungal properties can be used for such conditions as athlete's foot and other fungal infections. Since the oils also work on the brain via the sense of smell, they act on the emotions and they are very useful not only for stress-relief, but for anxiety and overwork, etc.

Because essential oils are very potent and have a physical effect, greater care is needed in their use than with the other vibrational therapies. Indeed, the use of some oils has a less than beneficial effect on children, pregnant women, or those subjected to epileptic fits, so it is as well to have a basic understanding of those which are safe to use in the home. The other caution is the need to buy pure and unadulterated essential oils and this is more important when they are to be used for therapeutic purposes. It is possible to buy oils ready blended in a carrier oil for general purposes, like baths, massage and room fragrances, and these do not require further dilution.

Some oils have relaxing and sedative properties, some are invigorating and it is possible to blend two or three oils together which often creates a synergistic effect more potent than using the oils singly.

The usual methods of using the oils are as follows:

Massage: The most common therapeutic form used by Aromatherapists, massage can be used in the home either by yourself in a limited form, or with the help of a friend or partner. It is a very effective way of reducing stress and tension and it encourages circulation and eases minor aches and pains. You can also rub blended oils locally into areas giving problems such as a stiff neck or wheezy chest. In self massage use gentle strokes towards the heart to encourage circulation. The essential oils diluted in a carrier oil, such almond or grapeseed, will be absorbed into the skin and then be diffused throughout the system, the fragrance directly reaching the brain through the olfactory senses, and the vibratory frequencies infusing the subtle energy fields of the body. The usual dilution is two drops of essential oil to 5ml (one teaspoon) of carrier oil. There is a possibility that further dilution has just as beneficial an effect, and always use a blend that you like the smell of.

Baths: Use a ready mixed blend or add two to five drops of pure essential oil to your bath, just before you get in. Stir the water to disperse the oils and do not use any other bath oil, salts or foam at the same time. For children, use only two drops in the bath.

Footbaths: Add two or three drops of oil into a bowl of hand-hot water and soak the feet for ten minutes.

Compresses: Use hot compresses for conditions such as backache, arthritic or rheumatic pain. Use cold compresses for recent injuries or acute conditions such as sprains, headaches, bruises or swelling. For hot compresses use water as hot as is comfortable, for cold compresses add ice to cold water. Add two or three drops of oil to the water, fold some lint and place it on the surface of the water so that it takes up the essential oil. Wring it out and apply where needed.

Inhalation: Use two to three drops of essential oil to one pint of water. Float the oil on the surface of the steaming water that is just off the boil. Drape a towel over your head and breathe the steam for two to three minutes.

Face and Hair Oil: Use one drop of essential oil to 10ml (two teaspoons) of carrier oil for a facial and body oil. For the hair, massage the blend into the scalp and leave for 15-30 minutes before shampooing.

On Tissues: For colds, headaches, general stuffiness, etc, put one drop of oil on to a tissue or handkerchief and inhale at intervals.

As a general rule do not apply neat essential oil onto your skin. Lavender and Tea-tree are two exceptions that can be used for the relief of insect bites and stings, using only one or two drops on a ball of cotton wool and dabbing gently.

Never ever take essential oils internally although this method is occasionally used by professionally qualified Aromatherapists. Always keep undiluted oils away from the eyes, from naked flames (they are inflammable) from plastics or polished wood surfaces and also take care if you are prone to allergic reactions to perfumes. Also do not use aromatherapy in conjunction with homeopathy as it is believed that strong aromas cancel the effects of some homeopathic remedies.

Essential oils deteriorate with time and are prone to the effects of light, oxygen, heat and moisture. It is wise to store them in a moderate temperature away from light. They are usually supplied in dark glass bottles and then boxed and it is best to store them in their boxes to help protect them from light. Citrus oils have the shortest shelf life - approximately one year.

When blended with vegetable carrier oils they do not keep for more than a couple of months. This is because they oxidise and turn rancid. Adding 5% Wheatgerm Oil (which is an anti-oxidant) helps keeping qualities, it is also excellent for dry skins.

Many plants which are processed for their essential oils are grown in herb gardens and herbs have provided humanity with many and varied benefits throughout the centuries. Herbs are plants which enhance our lives although the word herb usually refers to a smaller category of plants in the present day.

Throughout history, herbs were of great value and were as readily available to the peasants and common people as to the wealthy of the day, as they were plentiful and easy to collect and prepare.

From the earliest times herbs have been used for the health and well-being of humans and animals, frequently used to purify and sweeten the unhygenic environments in cities, and to disguise the taste of food which was less than wholesome.

Modern medicine owes much to the world of plants and herbs as many synthetic drugs are derived from plants initially, the active ingredient being chemically copied. The main difference between a drug and a herb used medicinally is that the active ingredient is only a very small part of the plant. The chemist ignores all the other parts of the plant, whereas the herbalist contends that the whole plant is necessary as it acts in a synergistic way thereby offsetting any negative effects that may be caused by the main active ingredient. This also means that they work more slowly than a drug, although there are obviously occasions when the fast action of a drug is required.

There was a long-held belief supported by many, including Paracelsus in the sixteenth century and Culpepper in the seventeenth century, which maintained that the appearance of a plant gave a sign or indication, either by shape, colour or scent, of the type of disease it would cure. This was known as the Doctrine of Signatures. There may be more to the idea than just simple superstition, as it is possible that plants and trees could be identified by the properties of their outward form in the same way that a crystal shape is determined by the energy patterns of its constituent atoms.

Another suggestion has been that the plant of each country may better cure the ills of the individuals living there.

To take this further it may be that the type of plants that naturally seed themselves in your garden are those which would be of benefit to you at that time, and when you no longer have need for that plant's healing energy the plant may no longer appear in your garden.

Herbalists, of course, work with a wide range of different herbs and train for many years to be well versed in their various effects. Some plants are dangerous and because we have not grown up with the accumulated wisdom earlier peoples had regarding plants and herbs, it is not wise for us to rush out into the countryside to collect plants for their therapeutic benefits. What we can do, however, is make use in the home of the common everyday herbs and spices generally considered for food use, then we know for sure that what we are using is totally safe.

Many of these herbs can be grown in the garden or even in pots on a sunny windowsill. Just being in the presence of herbs is generally beneficial, as their energy alone seems to be uplifting to the spirits. Herbs are strong and stable plants with fragrant and strong tasting leaves.

Spices are also often undervalued and can be very useful in the home for their therapeutic effects and I personally have cause to be grateful to the beneficial effects of Cayenne Pepper (used in conjunction with antibiotics prescribed by my doctor) which bought me much relief when used as a poultice and in a foot bath when I had a very severe chest infection.

Here is a list of herbs and spices and a brief note on their properties, some of which are compiled from an invaluable book called *Jennie's Little Book of Herb and Spice Remedies*, written by Dr. Jennie Charlston-Stokes.

Angelica: Good for children as it has a sweet taste. Used as a remedy for colds, coughs, respiratory disorders, rheumatism, indigestion and urinary disorders. A very versatile herb.

Basil: Has a pungent flavour and can improve the taste of many savoury dishes. Eases mild nervous disorders including headaches, nausea and travel sickness. Seems to help calm the mind and clear the head. Good for helping to clear warts, corns and verruccae - simply wash the feet with basil tea.

Dill:	Excellent for dispelling wind and for easing hiccoughs in young children. Has been used for centuries as the main constituent of gripe-water and soothing syrups.
Fennel:	Effective for stomach, spleen, pancreas, gall-bladder, liver and kidneys. Helps aid a sluggish metabolism, cleanses the breath and has blood cleansing properties. Is said to have the ability to restore failing vision and aids people who need to lose weight.
Garlic:	Considered to be the most effective antiseptic and blood purifier. Its main drawback being its pungent odour, however chewing an apple or eating a sprig of parsley helps to sweeten the breath. It is also considered a useful aid to the immune system and is an all embracing treatment for many ailments.
Marjoram:	Useful for soothing frayed nerves and is a stimulant which induces a gentle perspiration. Aids the digestion, liver upsets and gastric headaches and can help ease period pains. Can also soothe the lungs for those who have asthma, bronchitis or catarrh. Useful as a poultice for easing swellings and swollen joints, sprains and bruising.
Mint:	From the earliest records mint in all its forms has been used as a medicine for a range of complaints. Useful for abdominal pains, arthritis, acne, cramps, coughs, colds, colic, fevers, headaches, heartburn, insomnia, itching, menstrual problems including PMT, nausea, rheumatism, stress and tension. It is considered one of the finest oxygenators of the bloodstream and helps heal all circulatory diseases.

Parsley: Cools the blood by regulating its acidity which in
                turn soothes the nerve centres of the head and
                spine, thereby lowering the blood pressure,
                expels surplus fluid from the body tissues and
                acts as a natural antibiotic against infections. It
                also has strong deodourising properties and has
                a high iron and mineral content, helpful for
                alleviating anaemia and menstrual complaints.

Rosemary: Meaning 'Dew of the Sea' - is a common food
                medicine, considered a 'woman's herb' as it
                brings relief from hormonal problems and helps
                the fatigue associated with the menopause. It is
                also said to revitalise the brain and is good for
                alleviating nervous tension and depression and
                stimulates the appetite and nervous system.

Sage: The ancients said that sage brought an active
                long life and is one of the best tonics available.
                It has blood cleansing properties and is a
                genuine natural 'pick me up'. Mixed with cider
                vinegar it is good for coughs, colds and catarrh
                and is a very effective mouthwash and gargle.

Thyme: An effective insect repellent that is also good at
                lifting the spirits. Alleviates skin itches and aids
                sore and sweaty feet. It is another good tonic,
                mouthwash and gargle and is excellent for
                treating coughs and colds, circulation problems
                and digestive problems of all kinds. A very
                versatile herb.

Among the spices, a few to mention are:

Cayenne: A powerful local stimulant ideally applied as a
                poultice or ointment, however keep away from
                sensitive areas. It can also be used in a footbath
                for colds, flu and chest complaints and is good as
                a general stimulant that helps to build up

resistance. It is a powerful antiseptic and is also good for digestive disorders. Stimulates the appetite and helps in cases of loss of taste. Increases poor circulation and is helpful for the relief of rheumatism.

Cloves: Have antiseptic and germicidal properties. Good for alleviating the pain caused by teething and toothache. A pinch of powdered cloves in a teaspoon of honey can be rubbed on sore and inflamed gums to cool and soothe. Cloves made into an ointment are also good for warming and soothing pains caused by chilled or cramped muscles, rheumatism, sciatica, etc., but never use on broken, or tender skin.

Ginger: Used since ancient times to delight the palate and soothe the stomach and digestive tract. It eases the throat and chest, cleanses the system of parasites and infections, warms and relaxes when chilled, and is good as a preventative measure against tummy upsets and travel sickness.

Mustard: Useful as a poultice for aches and pains and in foot baths. Never use on broken skin. Good for chest complaints and particularly useful for relieving arthritis, rheumatism, sciatica and spondylitis.

Pepper: This is a hot remedy whose action is to cool the system. Black pepper is a valuable remedy for diarrhoea and for cleansing the intestines. It also helps to regulate blood pressure and eases vertigo and nausea. It is also detoxifying and helpful for the digestive system.

These herbs and spices offer us simple and effective methods of self-healing but like all foods they deserve to be treated with respect and moderation.

Of course, there are many more herbs that can be grown in the herb garden specifically for medicinal use and many that are available to purchase dried ready for use, or in the form of teas or made into tablets.

We also need to briefly consider food in general for therapeutic benefit. The old adage 'You are what you eat' is very pertinent in these modern times where so much of our food is processed and adulterated.

It is possible nowadays to buy a whole range of pills containing vitamins and minerals which are designed to supplement our generally inadequate diets, and whilst these are useful it is a pity that we find ourselves unable to supply all our nutritional needs from the food we grow or buy to eat. The further complication of additives, pesticides and insecticides only adds to the problem, and the growing use of convenience foods and the 'fast food' mentality aggravates the situation.

I am not a nutritionist so I can only suggest as a general guideline for optimum health we find sources of fresh, preferably organic vegetables and fruit, use wholemeal bread when possible, and eat organic and humanely reared meat if available. Freshly grown sprouted seeds, such as alfalfa and bean sprouts are full of valuable nutrients and beans, pulses, potatoes, noodles and pastas are also beneficial as are vegetable oils, fish, eggs and a moderate amount of dairy products. Raw vegetables or vegetables that are cooked quickly, as in the stir fry method, or steamed, will be generally better for you than those over cooked.

I would also suggest that it is not just the quality and freshness of food that is important but the 'atmosphere' in which food is prepared. Given our growing awareness of the subtle energies and vibrations it may be beneficial to consider that the food prepared in a harmonious environment, with love and care, is going to do us more good than food prepared by someone angry or resentful. It is also more beneficial to eat food in a harmonious atmosphere, free from any negative emotional states. You are probably aware of how difficult it is to eat if you are upset, anxious or under great stress. In fact under these circumstances we usually lose our appetite completely.

Before leaving this Chapter on Healing in the Home, I would like to briefly mention the therapeutic effects of having a pet. Our relationship with animals can often allow us to feel love from the heart and it has been discovered that many patients suffering from heart complaints will have increased life expectancy when they have a loving relationship with a pet. The very act of stroking a cat or dog appears to be beneficial to both the human and the animal and the unconditional love animals have the capacity for often gives us great psychological benefit. We often get to rely on our pets emotionally and turn to them in times of stress for relief or refuge. Pets can be of great emotional importance to children, the elderly, and other vulnerable groups of people.

Overall then, whilst we do obviously need the support and availability of modern health care and medicines, there is much to be said for taking some measure of responsibility for our own well-being and these simple, yet effective, methods, tried and tested over many years, are readily available to all of us.

CHAPTER 11

HEALING GARDENS

A garden is a sacred place. The concept of the Garden of Eden as humanity's point of origin is echoed by the idea of the garden representing our home-coming. Throughout history the garden has been central in the spiritual quest for paradise and this theme has appeared in many of the world's religions.

The earth itself represents the garden in macrocosm, with each individual garden the microcosm, The garden is our personal interface with nature, our window on the natural world. To many the garden is a sanctuary, peaceful, soothing and yet inspiring.

For centuries gardens have been created for varying purposes. The Egyptians and Mesopotamians planted gardens for shade beside their houses and grew plants for food and to flavour meat. By 1500 BC the Egyptians grew flowers for decoration. China has an ancient history of gardens that grew medicinal herbs. The Assyrians and Babylonians cultivated large parks for pleasure and hunting and the Persians further developed gardens and created their famous 'Paradise Gardens'. The Greeks created courtyard gardens with plants and statues and the Romans firmly established gardens as an integral part of the home.

The Aztecs of Mexico had a passion for decorative flowers and they developed floating gardens and elaborate terraced gardens. The Medieval Herb Gardens of the European Monasteries evolved into Physic Gardens such as the Chelsea Physic Garden opened in London in 1673 which still exists today.

The French developed a passion for grand formal gardens which spread to Britain, although by the 18th Century landscaped gardens by such notables as Capability Brown became popular.

Humanity's relationship with plants is also ancient. Trees and plants provided early people with many benefits and nearly all parts of the plant would be used, for food, medicine, cloth and fibre, shelter, dyes etc. Green plants are the builders and producers who convert the energy of sunlight via the process of photosynthesis which takes in carbon dioxide from the atmosphere and releases oxygen back into the atmosphere, after converting the carbon into its own cells.

There is an amazing diversity of richness in the plant world which we tend to ignore in our modern world, forgetting that this diversity is vital for the survival of the earth and for all who exist upon her.

Today the classification of herb only applies to a fraction of the plants. Originally herbs were any plant that was of use or value to us and many flowers and vegetables fall into this category. A garden full of herbs in their widest sense is a place full of life, colour, fragrance, texture, shape and form. Just by being in a garden which is full of vitality is enough to bring healing to our hearts and minds and our subtle energies are impacted upon by the vibrations and frequencies of the life-enhancing herbs.

Many garden designers work on the principle of designing a garden as if it were an extra room and although they have a good understanding of the plants' needs and requirements, and a grasp of good design principles, only a few see the garden as a dynamic whole on an energy level or in terms of healing. So what elements can we bring together to create a healing garden?

One of the first elements is the requirement for the garden to be organic. By definition a garden that uses chemical fertilisers and poisonous herbicides and insecticides, cannot be life-enhancing. Even from a subtle energy point of view, these substances are not going to interact with us beneficially. We also need to remember that we depend absolutely on the living soil. Most soils are teeming with life - a single spoonful may contain a million bacteria and miles of fungal filaments, and a few shovelfuls may contain 1000 different 'species'. A huge range of soil processors supply plants with all the fertility they require by making nutrients available from mineral particles. When the plants are removed from the soil the nutrients are removed too, therefore, they must be replaced with organic matter so that the processors are well nourished and can carry out their role. Because of this we need to feed the soil, not the plant.

The natural process of nutrient release is often too slow for the modern day gardener which is why so many are tempted to bypass the natural system altogether and to provide the plants directly with soluble nutrients, usually in the form of chemical fertilisers. Eventually the soil itself will lose its natural fertility. Soil fertility is not just a matter of nutrients, it is a combination of chemical, physical and biological factors such as soil texture, composition, structure, pH levels and a thriving community of organisms. The best way to address soil fertility in the garden is by the addition of organic matter.

There are three methods of adding organic matter to the soil. You can grow green manures, for example legumes or clovers (green manures are plants that as they grow fix nitrogen into the soil). You can introduce fresh plant material from elsewhere, either digging it in or using it as a mulch, or you can "pre-digest" the organic matter in a compost heap before adding it to the soil.

There are many good books available on the subject of organic gardening which I suggest you refer to.

The other aspect of organic gardening is the control of diseases and pests. The conventional answer to pests is the use of chemical pesticides but, particularly in the garden, it makes more sense not to use such poisons. The appearance of pests and so called weeds in the garden is an indication of the lack of balance inherent in most gardens. For the majority of pests there is a natural predator so we need to create as many different kinds of habitats and microclimates as possible to attract many kinds of wildlife, and to plant as many members of the daisy and carrot family whose small and open flowers provide nectar for the adults of insect species which have predatory larvae. Tolerate a variety of weeds and wild plants, these have grown in response to a lack of certain nutrients which your garden obviously needs. These wild plants will often have a cleansing effect in their own right. Also, bare soil loses more moisture so will have a natural tendency to 'cover itself up'.

Look at the concept of companion planting, the most well known being the planting of garlic with roses which helps protect the roses from aphid attack. Companion planting is basically the use of sympathetic energy relationships between plants to naturally stimulate their growth by placing them alongside each other. John Davidson in his book 'Subtle Energy' mentions a botanist called George Benner and a Dr. Philbrick who were both interested in the concept of companion planting. Using methods proposed by Rudolph Steiner over sixty years ago certain experiments were carried out using the sap from plants which was added to a 5% solution of copper chloride and allowing the mixture to dry into a crystalline pattern. The pattern for each plant was found to be both repeatable and unique - giving in effect a 'fingerprint' of each plant's energies. Interestingly if the sap from two plants were used, then the pattern was either harmonious or disharmonious. According to this research the plants that are good companions show harmonious patterns, whilst those not in harmony show disharmonious patterns in their crystalline structures.

Benner continued this research by mixing a drop of saliva with the 5% copper chloride solution. Remarkably the saliva of patients seemed to have a distinctive fingerprint and those with particular conditions reminded him of certain herbal crystalline patterns. This herbal pattern appeared to belong to the herb which would be used to treat that particular condition. Perhaps the body is requesting that vibration in order to heal itself. If this is so then this whole subject warrants much investigation and gives further recognition to the importance of herbs, and their vibrations, in our lives.

To get back to the garden, what other elements are necessary to create a healing environment? We briefly mentioned attracting wildlife to keep down pests but we also benefit in other ways from having a rich diversity of wildlife in our gardens. Like the spider's web, a garden is an interconnecting web of energies, patterns and relationships and the more we attract wildlife the more diversity and richness we bring into our lives. Paradoxically, modern farming methods have forced wildlife into gardens which have become a refuge for birds, mammals, reptiles and insects. Grow nectar rich plants for bees, butterflies and moths; provide a pond and wetland area for fish, frogs, toads and newts; plant hedgerow plants which provide berries and fruits for birds and small mammals; trees and shrubs to provide shade and nesting areas; logs and stumps or a woodpile that can rot and provide a habitat for insects. A box full of straw in a woodland area will attract hedgehogs who are territorial, into your garden, and if you are really fortunate you may see foxes and badgers in the dark of the night.

Consider the colour you use in your garden, which can create mood and ambience - do you prefer hot zingy colours, restful blues and purples, or neutral greens. Also consider the special effects given by white, or creamy, flowers in the garden. Many white flowers are very fragrant and white becomes almost luminous at dusk when the light begins to fail and gives a magical effect to any garden. Indeed, in that period when the light just starts to think about fading, all the colours in your garden will take on a particular beauty. This is the time of day when light starts to meet dark and colour comes wonderfully alive.

To cater for the sense of touch, texture is all important. Certain plants have leaves with incredible textures, some have smooth leaves or rubbery and waxy leaves. Several plants have leaves that are decidedly woolly, reminding you of cat's ears or mohair. The plants in the succulent family often have leaves which are cold to touch, such as the 'ice' plants.

Trees can often have interesting bark textures, some of which shed their bark like the Betula Papyrifera, a birch which sheds it very tactile bark.

Many flowers and seedheads are wonderfully tactile, the petals of a rose, for example, are unsurpassed for their softness. Seedheads are often extraordinarily light or may have a papery texture.

Touching plants and herbs, the leaves in particular, is also the best way to enjoy the fragrance of a plant. Crushing a leaf of Mint, Lemon Balm, Lavender or Verbena, releases the essences within the cells of leaves and the fragrance is cleansing and uplifting. Many scented plants do not have strong colours as they utilise the fragrance instead of the colour to attract pollinators.

Night scented flowers are mostly white or cream coloured and often have tubular flowers adapted to long tongued pollinators searching for nectar and their fragrance is only given off in the cooler temperatures of evening when the flowers open fully.

One way to enjoy the fragrance of plants whilst relaxing in your garden is to plant a scented climbing plant on a frame or trellis around a garden seat creating a bower. These bowers were very popular in Medieval times and scented roses, honeysuckles, jasmines and wisteria could be used to provide colour, texture and fragrance.

From a visual point of view also consider shape, form and structure in your garden. Many garden designers refer to this as the 'bones' of a garden and this becomes particularly important during the winter months. Landscape features such as walls, terraces, paths, pergolas etc, provide a basic framework and you can also use hedges, trees and shrubs. You may wish to design a framed view by putting in a gate or a 'window' in a wall. The circular 'window' often found in Chinese gardens was called a Moongate and could be created using wood, brick or stone.

Containers can also be used, terracotta pots, urns, old sinks, cartwheels, etc can all be utilised at the intersections of paths or against walls. You might like to consider creating a sunken garden that has the added benefit of keeping out the wind. There are many possibilities if you use your imagination.

We have already looked at the effect that sound has on our well-being and in the garden there are many sounds that can help alleviate the stress of the modern world. The song of the birds, humming of bees and insects on a summer's day are all soothing sounds. The movement of wind through trees and shrubs is pleasing and you can plant bamboo and tall grasses to create rustling sounds. To emphasise the sound of the breeze use windchimes, bells, streamers etc.

The sound of running water in a garden is a tranquil sound. Waterfalls and fountains, even small ones, are a lovely addition to any garden, and if you really love the idea of water in your garden create a large pool or meandering stream. The Japanese have some lovely ideas for water gardens and water seems to energise a garden in a particularly special way.

Finally, you may wish to create your entire garden, or some part of it, to a particular theme - a romantic garden, a herb garden, a formal garden or perhaps a secret garden. Or if not an overall theme you may wish to add symbols to your garden. A sundial, statue of a pagan deity, an astrological herb wheel, a small maze or labyrinth, sculpture, a shell garden, topiary, a Japanese lantern, a rock garden - all of these can have meanings on a symbolic level and help personalise your garden.

You may feel drawn to the idea of creating a traditional Japanese Garden which were usually designed to be contemplative, meditative and strongly symbolic. Water and stone are the two main features of a Japanese Garden but it is the skill of composition that is most important. The Zen Buddhists in Japan developed the art of so-called dry gardens which were originally designed for contemplation by monks and made little use of plants. These gardens were usually walled and featured sand or small stones raked into different patterns to represent flowing water with large stones placed to represent mountains. The raking of the sand or stones was considered an act of worship and is quite therapeutic in its own way.

In the late evenings of summer, gardens can become quite magical places. You may wish to add subtle outdoor lighting to enhance the magical effect or you may find time just to experience the beauty of a garden on a night with a full moon.

By definition a garden is a place where we may feel that we have tamed nature, it is a haven and a sanctuary from the cares of our own lives and from the 'wildness' of nature in the raw. In a way we may lose something in the process and find that to make the strongest connection with nature and the earth, we need to go out into 'the wild blue yonder', the wilderness - to walk in deep forests, climb hills or mountains, walk by the seashore or be out in the wildness of a thunderstorm, to appreciate the sheer force and beauty of nature. At times we do need the larger connection but a garden does provide us with a point of 'first contact' where we can perhaps actively work and co-operate with the energies and intelligences inherent within nature.

In 1962 a couple called Peter and Eileen Caddy moved to a Caravan Park on the windswept dunes of Findhorn Bay in Morayshire, Scotland. Peter was a former Squadron Leader in the Royal Air Force and had for many years followed a spiritual path. Eileen, his wife, was also somewhat clairvoyant and together with their children and a friend, Dorothy Maclean, also a sensitive, they gradually realised that their purpose at this inhospitable site was to create a garden. This eventually became the Findhorn Garden that attracted attention and visitors from around the world, who came to marvel at the wonderful variety and remarkable healthiness of the vegetables, trees, fruits and flowers.

Their 'guidance' had come from the intelligence inherent in nature which helped them with specific gardening problems and gave them many helpful suggestions. This co-creative partnership enhanced the garden and achieved remarkable results. They called the individual intelligences within species of plants Devas after the Sanskrit word meaning 'Shining Ones'. The Devas appeared to be the form builders or architects of the plant world, who brought forth the blueprint for each species at the start of their 'New Year'. When this blueprint was finalised the next level down in the etheric realms took over the process of bringing fully into form the individual plants. This level was referred to as the Nature Spirit level, organised by the 'head nature spirit' a being they called Pan after the Greek god of nature.

The information they received was usually specific and practical, involving the making of good quality compost, the depth of planting, the space each plant required, the amount of water they needed, etc, which resulted in crops and plants that were free from disease, full of vitality and energy, bursting with the life-force and hence were extremely nourishing.

Inspired by the events at Findhorn, Machaelle Small Wright from Virginia, USA, who was already working with organic methods of gardening, created and developed a method of gardening called Co-creative Gardening in her 100 foot diameter circular garden called Perelandra.

Perelandra became a Nature Research Centre and Machaelle with the support of her husband, Clarence, has developed practical ideas on how anyone can, if they wish, work with the intelligence within nature, details of which can be found in the two Garden Workbooks written by Machaelle (see address for Perelandra at end of book). This Co-creative Gardening results in a garden that is balanced in every respect, from the soil on and below the ground, to the air and atmosphere above it, the plants, insects and animals, all creating a dynamic whole that simply radiates an energy of well-being.

This does not happen straight away - in fact it took a few years for the level of balance to be achieved, but with nature's input there has never been any need for chemical fertilisers, pesticides, insecticides, etc, and the plants grown are strong and full of nourishment. Pests do exist but are usually contained in a small area because even pests are part of the overall balance and energy of a Co-creative Garden.

Not all of us feel the desire to work with nature in this way, and many will reject the concept completely, but some of us may be inspired to at least see nature in a new light and work in the garden with a spirit of co-operation that will go a long way to healing our relationship with the natural world and the earth we live upon.

CHAPTER 12

"BLESS THIS HOUSE"

Nature is an intricate web where everything is interrelated and our homes too are a microcosm of interrelated energies comprising of the physical components, the people, and the accumulated thoughts and feelings of the people who live there.

In past times when people 'saw' spirits dwelling in all places, the home would have had its own spirits, including those of its inhabitants' ancestors, who acted as guardians. In Eastern Europe, house spirits were referred to as "grandfather" and "grandmother", as a sign of respect for their wisdom and age. In cultures as diverse as Rome and West Africa, ancestral spirits would be symbolically represented by masks. Through these masks the ancestors would look upon us and if the masks could be worn, we could symbolically take the ancestors place.

There were the guardian spirits of the threshold, the place where inside and outside meet traditionally being a magical place. There were also hearth guardians who were usually female, whereas the threshold guardians were usually male.

The most famous household spirits were the Lares of the Romans. The Lares were both household and family deities and were consulted on family affairs on a daily basis and given offerings of flour and salt.

In the Middle Ages, and even more recently than that, sacrifices were made when houses were built, to appease the household spirits. These sacrifices were sometimes of fruit and grains, or newly laid fertile eggs, but often were animals, particularly cats. There were also ceremonies conducted at the laying of the foundation stone and the topping out ceremony when the roof was completed. Such ceremonies are still continued to this day, but we tend to do without the sacrifice.

The Saxons would place antlers at the ends and peaks of their roofs for protection and in the medieval era, iron was used to safeguard the home. Lengths of chain, forkheads or possibly swords were all used under the foundations of the house and iron horseshoes were placed above the door lintel for protection. For households the prongs were in an upright position to hold in the luck, whereas it was only in the Blacksmith's Forge where horseshoes could be hung with the prongs pointing down, to pour out the luck onto the forge.

Certain trees were also planted outside the house, particularly on both sides of the entrances for protection. Elder, Rowan, Bay and Hawthorn were popular choices.

In times past it was recognised that cleansing was required not only on the physical level, but on an inner level too. The accumulation of energy from angry words and thoughts, dark desires, constant arguing or negatives thoughts and feelings can be 'held' in the very fabric of the house, giving rise to a 'bad atmosphere' or even a reputation for hauntings.

The long established ritual of Spring Cleaning had magical overtones as Spring was symbolic of the Earth's renewal and as such was the ideal time to cleanse the home and welcome the energies of the new season. A brief ritual associated with Spring Cleaning was to open all the windows and doors to air the house, then light a white candle which had been rubbed with a floral oil such as rose. Sprigs of scented leaves or flowers were placed before the candle and after a few moments of meditating on the home being cleansed, the Spring Cleaning was commenced whilst the candle was still safely burning.

It was also considered appropriate to go around the outside of the house and the borders or boundary of the property, sprinkling water or corn to bless the home. The borders of a village would be honoured by the villagers in a custom called "Beating the Bounds". Once a year the whole village would process around the boundaries, beating landmarks and cornerstones with sticks to help redefine their village. In some cases the children were whipped or ducked in cold water which was supposed to help them to remember exactly where the boundaries were.

In Pagan rituals the elements would be used to cleanse the house, salt for the element of earth, blessed water for the element of water, candles for the element of fire and incense for the element of air. When using each element, they would be addressed in turn, thus:

By the Powers of Earth, I Cleanse This House

After such a ritual noise would often be used as part of the cleansing and drums, bells, rattles and horns would all be used as noise was believed to disturb any harmful spirits.

Another traditional custom still practised today is the Housewarming Party where you introduce your friends to your new house. The gifts they bring should always be for the house and not for you and much eating, drinking and merrymaking fills the new home with positive energy.

It may be that even in this day and age, when you move into a new home, you may wish to acknowledge in some way the clearing of old energies, particularly in an old house. Physically cleaning the house is a start and you may like to use candles and incense and the power inherent in words to show your intent to cleanse the home on an inner and outer level.

In the Perelandra Garden in America, information received directly from the intelligence inherent in Nature, suggests that Nature itself is capable of acting as a buffer by absorbing a lot of the negative thoughts and feelings in our environment. This appears to be why forests and woods are so important, particularly situated near to towns and cities as they act as giant stabilisers on the emotional level and in a sense give us time to handle the effects of too much negative emotion.

It is also suggested that during times of war where there is almost an overload of negative emotions, Nature absorbs a lot of this excess which is released gradually over a period of time. This could be why some sensitive people experience ancient, and not so ancient, battles taking place on old battlefields in the present time. During a major war such as World War I, the overload was probably so great that even Nature had a difficult time trying of offset its effects, thus when the war ended, a devastating flu epidemic killed more people than the war itself and this was possibly caused by the accumulated effects of the negative energies released by the fear and horror of the war.

The ability of Nature to absorb such energies also gives us another reason why it is such a good idea to bring plants, flowers and crystals into our homes, as these natural, living, 'things' are capable of absorbing and offsetting the effects of disharmony and discord which they help to transmute over a period of time. Fresh air and sunshine are also two important aspects of Nature which can help cleanse on both an inner and outer level.

As all homes are sometimes subjected to discord as well as the energies that are broadcasted into the home from radio and television, you may wish to consider cleansing your home in this way on a regular basis.

Another powerful antidote to any lingering, unpleasant energies is laughter, so fill your home with the sound of laughter as often as you can.

And finally ....

I have deliberately avoided giving a room by room analysis of furnishings and decor as this is where your own abilities and creativity come into play. Your home is a place where you can choose the way you want to live, you do not need that choice made for you by 'experts'. By all means study the influences of the past and the fashions of the present. You may feel more comfortable with Neo-Classicism, Regency, Victorian or Edwardian styles, or you may wish to experiment with an eclectic, modern, country or ethnic style, but whatever you choose remember that taste is a personal thing and we should celebrate our differences. Only we know what we really like.

I think that taste is a matter of resonance. Something you like resonates at a similar, or harmonious, frequency to you, whether it be a colour, sound, object, pattern, an animal or plant, or a person, they just 'feel right'. We may be drawn to natural surroundings, colourful areas, or prefer a more formal or even high-tech approach, but even in the most technological of environments, if we are to avoid becoming alienated, we still need to be connected in some way with nature and with the greater environment.

We also need to learn to take what is best from the ideas of the past, many of which have worked well through centuries, and marry them to a visionary future. A future where technology appropriately serves our needs, and where we each become empowered individuals, fully aware that to become whole we need to have a sense of our place in the scheme of things, a sense of our own self-worth, confidence and belief in our own abilities, until the day we leave this earth and journey to that final home-coming.

RESOURCES

Architects/Designers

Ecological Design Association
Slad Road
Stroud
Glos
GL5 1QW
01453 765575

Organic Paints/Finishes

Auro Organic Paints
Unit 1
Goldstone Farm
Ashdon
Saffron Walden
Essex
CB10 2LZ
01799 584888

Self Build

Walter Segal Self Build Trust
57 Chalton Street
London
NW1 1HU
0171 388 9582

Colour/Full Spectrum Lighting

Living Colour Institute
33 Lancaster Grove
London
NW3 4EX
0171 794 1371

Hygeia Studios
Colour Light Art Research Ltd
Brook House
Avening
Tetbury
Glos
GL8 8NS
01453 832150

New Age Music

Dawn Awakening Music Ltd
Foxhole
Dartington
Totnes
Devon
TQ9 6EB
01803 864822

World Music

Labyrinth Distribution
2 Hargrave Place
London
N7 0BP
0171 267 6154

Tibetan Singing Bowls

Alain Rouveure
Crossing Cottage Galleries
Todenham
Nr. Moreton-in-Marsh
Glos
GL56 9NU
01608 650418

Feng Shui

Feng Shui Network International
Lazenby House
2 Thayer street
London
W1M 5LG
0171 935 8935

Incense (Mail Order)

Maksha
7 Hillview
Churchill
Oxon
OX7 6ND
01608 658937

Flow Forms

John Wilkes
Virbela Flow Design Research Group
Emerson College
Forest Row
Sussex
RH18 5JX

Crystals (Mail Order)

Kernowcraft Rocks & Gems Ltd
Bolingey
Perranporth
Cornwall
TR6 0DH
01872-573888

Flower Remedies/Essences

The Bach Centre
Mount Vernon
Sotwell
Wallingford
Oxon
OX10 0PZ
01491 834678

The Flower & Gem Remedy Association
Suite 1
Castle Farm
Clifton Road
Deddington
Oxon
OX15 0TP
01869 337349

Greenman Tree Essences
2 Kerswell Cottages
Exminster
Exeter
Devon
EX6 8AY
01392 832005

Organic Gardening

Henry Doubleday Research Association
National Centre for Organic Gardening
Ryton on Dunsmere
Coventry
CV8 3LG
01203 303517

Co-Creative Gardening

Perelandra
PO Box 3603
Warrenton
VA 22186
USA

The Findhorn Foundation
The Park
Findhorn
Forres
Scotland
IV36 0TZ

Lazaris Audio Tapes

Susan Duffy
CLoud Nine
19 Eskburn Road
Tuebrook
Liverpool
L13 8BP
0151 226 9771

BIBLIOGRAPHY

The Natural House Book, David Pearson, A Gaia Original, Conran Octopus Ltd, London, 1989

Healing Environments, Carol Venolia, Celestial Arts, Berkeley, California, USA, 1988

Earth to Spirit, David Pearson, Gaia Books Ltd, London, 1994

Legendary Britain, Bob Stewart and John Matthews, Blandford Press, London, 1989

Subtle Energy, John Davidson, C.W. Daniel Co Ltd, Saffron Walden, 1987

Lifestyle, Your Surroundings and How They Affect You, Dr. Peter Marsh, Sidgwick & Jackson Ltd, London, 1990

Sacred Geometry, Nigel Pennick, Capall Bann Publishing, Newbury, 1994

Labyrinths, Ancient Myths & Modern Uses, Sig Lonegren, Gothic Image Publications, Glastonbury, 1991

Sacred Places, James A. Swan, Bear 7 Co, Sante Fe, New Mexico, USA, 1990

Earth Harmony, Nigel Pennick, Century Paperbacks, London, 1987

Sacred Architecture, A.T. Munro, Element Books Ltd, Shaftesbury, Dorset, 1993

Places of the Soul, Christopher Day, The Aquarian Press, Thorsons Publishing Group, Wellingborough, 1990

Surfers of the Zuvuya, José Argüelles, Bear & Co, Sante Fe, New Mexico, USA, 1989

Learn To See, Mary Jo McCabe, Blue Dolphin Publishing Inc, Nevada City, USA, 1994

The Future of Light, Hardwin Tibbs, Watkins Publishing, Dulverton, Somerset, 1981

Healing Through Colour, Theo Gimbel, D.C.E., C.W. Daniel Co Ltd, Saffron Walden, 1980

Form, Sound, Colour and Healing, Theo Gimbel, C.W. Daniel Co Ltd, Saffron Walden, 1987

The Rainment of Light, David Tansley, Routledge & Kegan Paul Plc, London, 1984

Fragrant & Radiant Healing Symphony, Roland Hunt, H.G. White, 1937

The Seven Keys of Colour Healing, Roland Hunt, C.W. Daniel Co Ltd, Saffron Walden, 1971

Colour Psychology & Colour Therapy, Faber Birren, The Citadel press, Secaucus, NJ, USA, 1961

The Principles of Light & Colour, Edwin Babbitt, The Citadel Press, Secaucus, NJ, USA, 1967

Colour & Personality, Audrey Kargere, Philosophical Library, USA, 1979

What Colour Are You? Annie Wilson & Lilla Bek, Turnstone Press Ltd, Wellingborough, 1981

The Ancient Art of Colour Therapy, Linda Clark, Simon & Schuster Division, New York, USA, 1975

The Healing Power of Colour, Betty Wood, Aquarian Press, Wellingborough, 1989

Know Yourself Through Colour, Marie Louise Lacy, Aquarian Press, Wellingborough, 1989

Handbook of the Aura, Laneta Gregory & Geoffrey Treissman, Pilgrims Book Services, Norwich, 1985

Sound Therapy, Heal Yourself with Music and Voice, Olivea Dewhurst-Maddock, Gaia Books Ltd, London, 1993

Music, Its Secret Influence throughout the Ages, Cyril Scott, The Aquarian Press, Wellingborough, 1958

Healing Music, Andrew Watson & Nevill Drury, Prism Press, Bridport, 1987

Interior Design with Feng Shui, Sarah Rossbach, Rider & Co, London, 1987

Supernature, Lyall Watson, Coronet Books, Hodder & Stoughton, London, 1973

Aromatherapy for Everyone, Robert Tisserand, Penguin Group, London, 1988

The Secret Life of Plants, Peter Tomkins and Christopher Bird, Penuin Books Ltd, Middlesex, 1973

Pot Pourri, Ann Tucker Tettner, Hutchinson & Co Ltd, London 1983

The Complete Book of Flowers, Denise Diamond, North Atlantic Books, California, USA, 1990

The Secret Lore of Plants & Flowers, Eric Maple, Robert Hale Ltd, London, 1980

Crystal Clear - A Guide to Quartz Crystal, Jennifer Dent, Capall Bann Publications, Newbury, 1994

Living Water, Olof Alexandersson, Gateway Books, Bath, 1990

The Magic of Perfume, Eric Maple, The Aquarian Press, Wellingborough, 1973

Gem Elixers & Vibrational Healing, Vol II, Gurudas, Cassandra Press, Boulder, Colorado, USA, 1986

Subtle Aromatherapy, Patricia Davis, C.W. Daniel Co Ltd, Saffron Walden, 1991

Homeopathy for the Family, Wigmore Publications Ltd, London, 1981

Healing Without Medicine, Jeremy Kingston, Aldus Books Ltd, London, 1976

Handbook of the Bach Flower Remedies, Philip M. Chancellor, C.W. Daniel Co Ltd, Saffron Walden, 1971

A Guide to the Bach Flower Remedies, John Barnard, C.W. Daniel & Co Ltd, Saffron Walden, 1979

The Art of Aromatherapy, Robert Tisserand, C.W. Daniel Co Ltd, Saffron Walden, 1977

Practical Aromatherapy, Shirley Price, Thorsons Publishers Ltd, Wellingborough, 1973

The Book of Herbs, Dorothy Hall, Pan Book Ltd, London, 1983

Jennie's Little Book of Herbs and Spice Remedies, Dr. Jennie Charlston-Stokes, Universal Press, Huntingdon

Booklet - Aromatherapy A-Z of Using Oils at Home, published by Here's Health (EMAP Elan Ltd) in conjunction with the Institute of Classical Aromatherapy, London, 1993

The Healing Garden, Sue Mintor, Headline Book Publishing Plc, London, 1993

World of Herbs, Lesley Bremness, Ebury Press, London, 1990

The Natural Garden Book, Peter Harper with Jeremy Light and Chris Madsen, Gaia Books Ltd, London, 1994

The Psychic Garden, Mellie Uyldert, Thorsons Publishers Ltd, Wellingborough, 1980

The Fragrant Garden, John & Rosemary Hemphill, Bookmart Ltd, Leicester, 1991

The Garden Workbook, Machaelle Small Wright, Perelandra, Virginia, USA, 1987

The Findhorn Garden, The Findhorn Community, published jointly by Turstone Books, London & Wildwood House Ltd, London, 1975

The Enchanted Forest, Yvonne Aburrow, Capall Bann Publishing, Newbury, 1994

The Pagan Family, Ceisiwr Serith, Llewellyn Publications, St. Paul, Mn, USA, 1994

The Magical Household, Scott Cunningham & David Harrington, Llewellyn Publications, St. Paul, Mn, USA, 1987

Article - Rhythm of Life in the 1993 Womad Festival Programme by Mikey Dread

Article by Robin Heath, Chalice Magazine, Issue 11, Summer 1994

Article by Jeff Chitouras on Esoteric Sound & Colour in Gnosis Magazine, Spring 1993

Article by William Spear on An Introduction to Feng Shui in the Spring 1992 Issue of Kindred Spirit, Totnes, Devon

Article by Paul Houghton on Homoeopathy's New Frontiers in Mind, Body, Soul, Issue Sept/Oct 1994, Hall Park Publications Ltd, Bletchley

Audio Tapes: Healing: The Nature of Health Part I and Healing: The Nature of Health Part II, Lazaris, Concept Synergy Publishing, Beverley Hills, USA

INDEX

fragrance, 12, 100-102, 105, 117, 119-121, 136, 148, 151-152
Frank, 34, 85
Frankincense, 102, 135
full spectrum lighting, 47, 163

Gaia, 15, 98, 167-169
Garden of Eden, 146
Garlic, 141, 149
gem remedies, 132
Genius Loci, 18
geomancy, 15
geomantic amnesia, 18
geometry, 35, 37, 167
geopathic stress, 105-106
George Benner, 150
George Washington Carver, 117
Geranium, 102, 134
Gerhard Finkenbeiner, 82
Glass Harmonica, 82
Goethe, 75
golden mean, 34-35
Greece, 32, 81, 101
green, 17, 37, 46, 51-52, 54, 56-57, 61-67, 69, 71-72, 80, 85, 116-117, 132, 147, 149
green manures, 149
green thumb, 116

Hans Jenny, 76
healing, 2-5, 7-8, 10-12, 26, 29, 32, 38, 40, 48-49, 65, 69, 75, 79-83, 85, 101, 111-112, 122-126, 128-129, 139, 145-146, 148, 150, 155, 167-170
hearth, 27, 107, 157
hedgehogs, 151
herbalists, 139
herbs, 2, 32, 121, 132, 138-140, 143, 147-148, 150-151, 169
Hermes, 26
hertz, 76
hexahedron, 35, 37
Hibiscus, 115

home-coming, 5, 146, 161
homoeopathy, 170
horseshoes, 157
horticultural therapy, 114
hot springs, 111-112
houseplants, 104, 114
Housewarming, 159
hue, 49, 52, 56
hydrogen, 109-110, 128

I Ching, 90-91
icosahedron, 35, 37, 40
Ikebana, 119
Imbolc, 24
incense, 102-103, 158-159, 164
Indian Music, 81
inhalation, 137
ionisation, 100

Jacques Benveniste, 127
James Lovelock, 15, 97
japanese, 28, 111, 153
Jasmine, 102, 133
Jazz Music, 81
John D. Ott, 46
John Davidson, 150, 167
John Wilkes, 111, 164
Juniper, 134

Kepler, 35, 37
King Saul, 81

labyrinths, 17-18, 167
Lammas, 24-25
language of flowers, 118
Lares, 157
laughter, 1, 160
Lavender, 66-67, 100, 102, 120, 133, 137, 151
left brain, 31
Lemon, 61, 102, 135, 151
Lemuria, 82
Li, 90-91
light value, 49, 52, 54

right brain, 31
Robin Heath, 22, 170
Rose Quartz, 122-123
rose, 21, 102, 118, 122-123, 130-132, 134, 151, 158
Rosemary, 133, 142, 170
Ru-shr, 91
Rudolph Steiner, 33, 150
runes, 26

SAD, 44
Sage, 142
Sandalwood, 102, 135
saxons, 157
Schumann Waves, 108
Scriabin, 85
shrines, 28
simultaneous contrast, 56
Singing Bowls, 28, 81-82, 164
So, 2-3, 5-6, 8-11, 16-18, 22-23, 25, 29-30, 34, 38, 40, 44, 47-48, 51-52, 59-60, 62-63, 66-67, 72-73, 75-83, 86, 89, 91, 94-96, 98, 100-101, 107, 109, 112, 114-116, 119-120, 122, 124-126, 131-132, 136-137, 144, 148-150, 159-160
softwoods, 104
Solar Calendar, 22
solar power, 107
spectrum, 44, 46-48, 52, 72, 77, 163
spices, 59, 121, 139-140, 142-143
Spider Plant, 115
spiral, 2, 14, 17, 26, 34, 111
spirograph, 37
split-complementary, 54
Spring Cleaning, 158
springs, 110-112
square, 31-32, 35, 40, 94
subtle energies, 11-12, 73, 125, 127, 132, 144, 148
sulphur dioxide, 99

sun, 14, 20-21, 23, 26, 34, 43-46, 64, 98, 104, 106-108, 116, 119, 135
symbols, 17, 20, 25-29, 44, 94, 117, 153

Taoist, 88
Tea-tree, 133, 137
temperature, 72, 106, 115, 138
temple, 5, 32
tetrahedron, 35, 37, 40
Theo Gimbel, 40, 75, 84, 167
Theseus, 17-18
Thyme, 142
Tibet, 81
Ton Alberts, 37
Tony Pinkus, 128
totem pole, 116
triadic, 54
triangle, 35, 38
triangular conversion, 40-41
Troy Towns, 17
turquoise blue, 54, 56, 59, 69
Tzolkin, 23

ultraviolet, 44, 46-47

varnishes, 104-105
VDU's, 100, 108, 115
Vesica Piscis, 38-39
vibrational healing, 12, 85, 125, 169
Viktor Schauberger, 110
violet, 37, 51-52, 54, 56, 61, 65-66, 70-72, 122, 130
vitality globules, 98
Vitamin D, 44
Walter Segal, 7, 162

waterfalls, 80, 100, 153
wave power, 107
weather, 23, 98
white flowers, 151

Healing Homes
Home Study Course

Jennifer has designed a Home Study Course based on her book.

This comprehensive twelve-part course consists of assignments, both written and practical, and includes:

- Additional information

- Colour illustrations for the colour work

- A cassette tape of specially composed music by Eilish O'Malley

- Samples/leaflets where appropriate.

For details of the course, please write to Jennifer:

> c/o Capall Bann Publishing
> Freshfields
> Chieveley
> Berks
> RG20 8TF

About the Author

Jennifer describes herself as a Thinker and a Dreamer, who has spent the past twenty or so years exploring the nature of reality.

A passionate reader of books since childhood illness kept her at home for long periods of time, Jennifer's early interest in metaphysics was triggered by her father's death, a love of science fiction and a natural curiosity about 'life the universe and everything'.

A lover of nature, plants, flowers, herbs, crystals, colour, music, cats, Star Trek and all shades of purple, she has also studied various aspect of healing for many years.

Jennifer lives in Berkshire with her husband Rik and two half Siamese cats.

Steve Hounsome Meditation Tapes

From the author of 'Taming the Wolf- Full Moon Meditations', a range of excellent meditation tapes, using techniques and exercises proven in numerous courses. The tapes contain safe and effective meditations which can be used for personal and spiritual development, to promote greater awareness of the self or simply for relaxation and enjoyment.

Taming the Wolf - Full Moon Meditation Tape

This tape was designed to accompany the book 'Taming the Wolf'. Meditations are adaptable to the individual nature of each moon. Suitable for use at each full moon by groups or individuals.

Spirit seeker Relaxation Tape

Produced in response to an expressed need for physical and mental relaxation. Requiring no prior knowledge or experience, this tape is especially useful and effective for sufferers of stress, tension, worry, insomnia etc. It is also ideally suited to the maintenance of health and wellbeing during pregnancy, study and recovery.

Tape 1. Essential Meditations; a.. Grounding & Connecting b. Tree Meditation

This ideal beginner's tape gives a firm basis for all the other tapes in the series. People who have long had trouble with meditation, grounding and connecting have found it to be of great use.

Tape 2. The Sanctuary and Meeting Your Guide

Side one contains a guided visualisation which enables you to create and use your own special place or Sanctuary. This can be used as a place to receive healing or as a gateway to a deeper level of meditation.

Side two takes you back to your Sanctuary with the intention to meet your guide. It is necessary to become familiar with your Sanctuary first and the meditation may need to be repeated several times before you come fully into contact with your guide.

Tape 3. The Healing Ring and Purification Breath

Side one is designed to help with self healing. A ring is visualised which passes over the body, removing disease as it passes. It helps those needs of which you are subconsciously aware.

Side two contains a calming energizing and healing meditation. It is ideally suited to those in the process of cleansing themselves, perhaps by changing their diet or giving up smoking. It will also help you become more senstive to the needs of your body.

Tape 4. House Meditation and The Pink Bubble

Side one takes you on a guided journey which takes you to areas which symbolise your Mind, Body and Spirit and also your conscious, subconscious and every day selves. Symbolic items can be moved from one part of yourself to another.

Side two contains a visualisation which can help you to achieve your goals. It also helps you to understand them and how they change. A suitable symbol is visualised, enclosed in a pink bubble and released to the Universe.

Price £6.00 (inc VAT) + £1.00 p&p (within UK) Direct from Capall Bann
Freshfields , Chieveley, Berks, RG20 8TF

FREE DETAILED CATALOGUE

A detailed illustrated catalogue is available on request, SAE or International Postal Coupon appreciated. Titles are available direct from Capall Bann, post free in the UK (cheque or PO with order) or from good bookshops and specialist outlets. Titles currently available include:

Animals, Mind Body Spirit & Folklore
Angels and Goddesses - Celtic Christianity & Paganism by Michael Howard
Arthur - The Legend Unveiled by C Johnson & E Lung
Auguries and Omens - The Magical Lore of Birds by Yvonne Aburrow
Book of the Veil The by Peter Paddon
Caer Sidhe - Celtic Astrology and Astronomy by Michael Bayley
Call of the Horned Piper by Nigel Jackson
Cats' Company by Ann Walker
Celtic Lore & Druidic Ritual by Rhiannon Ryall
Compleat Vampyre - The Vampyre Shaman: Werewolves & Witchery by Nigel Jackson
Crystal Clear - A Guide to Quartz Crystal by Jennifer Dent
Earth Dance - A Year of Pagan Rituals by Jan Brodie
Earth Harmony - Places of Power, Holiness and Healing by Nigel Pennick
Earth Magic by Margaret McArthur
Enchanted Forest - The Magical Lore of Trees by Yvonne Aburrow
Familiars - Animal Powers of Britain by Anna Franklin
Healing Homes by Jennifer Dent
Herbcraft - Shamanic & Ritual Use of Herbs by Susan Lavender & Anna Franklin
In Search of Herne the Hunter by Eric Fitch
Inner Space Workbook - Developing Counselling & Magical Skills Through the Tarot
Kecks, Keddles & Kesh by Michael Bayley
Living Tarot by Ann Walker
Magical Incenses and Perfumes by Jan Brodie
Magical Lore of Cats by Marion Davies
Magical Lore of Herbs by Marion Davies
Masks of Misrule - The Horned God & His Cult in Europe by Nigel Jackson
Mysteries of the Runes by Michael Howard
Oracle of Geomancy by Nigel Pennick
Patchwork of Magic by Julia Day
Pathworking - A Practical Book of Guided Meditations by Pete Jennings
Pickingill Papers - The Origins of Gardnerian Wicca by Michael Howard
Psychic Animals by Dennis Bardens
Psychic Self Defence - Real Solutions by Jan Brodie
Runic Astrology by Nigel Pennick
Sacred Animals by Gordon MacLellan
Sacred Grove - The Mysteries of the Forest by Yvonne Aburrow
Sacred Geometry by Nigel Pennick
Sacred Lore of Horses The by Marion Davies
Sacred Ring - Pagan Origins British Folk Festivals & Customs by Michael Howard
Seasonal Magic - Diary of a Village Witch by Paddy Slade
Secret Places of the Goddess by Philip Heselton
Talking to the Earth by Gordon Maclellan
Taming the Wolf - Full Moon Meditations by Steve Hounsome
The Goddess Year by Nigel Pennick & Helen Field
West Country Wicca by Rhiannon Ryall
Witches of Oz The by Matthew & Julia Phillips

Capall Bann is owned and run by people actively involved in many of the areas in which we publish. Our list is expanding rapidly so do contact us for details on the latest releases.

Capall Bann Publishing, Freshfields, Chieveley, Berks, RG20 8TF